INTRODUCTION

Scrappiness is happiness!

I love that many fabrics get to come out and play in a scrappy quilt, and all of them get along swimmingly. In making the quilts for this book, I was able to use up leftover fabric pieces that I had saved up over the years. I was also able to reacquaint myself with fabrics in my stash that I had forgotten about. It was SO much fun—until it came time to clean up. But we won't talk about that.

Each project in this book was thoughtfully designed for quilters who want to dig into their own fabric scraps and stash, as well as quilters who want to exchange blocks or trade fabrics with friends. In either case, I hope happy are the quilters who make these scrappy quilts, and happy are the receivers of any quilts that are given as gifts.

Soli Deo Gloria,

Wendy Sheppard

TABLE OF CONTENTS

Inspiration

"Red anything is just lovely! I decided that a scrappy book has to have a red scrappy quilt." —Wendy Sheppard

WHO DRANK THE FRUIT PUNCH?

Quilted by Darlene Szabo of Sew Graceful Quilting

Red quilts are always visually striking and appropriate for all seasons. This quilt uses small red prints and white prints from your stash.

SKILL LEVEL

Confident Beginner

FINISHED SIZES

Quilt Size: 61" x 75"
Block Size: 13½" x 13½"
Number of Blocks: 20

Fruit Punch
13½" x 13½" Finished Block
Make 20

MATERIALS

- 2½ yards assorted red prints*
- 3 yards assorted white prints for blocks*
- 1⅜ yards white print for sashing and border*
- ¾ yard red print for binding*
- 5 yards backing*
- 69" x 83" batting*
- Thread*
- Basic sewing tools and supplies

**Scrap fabrics from various collections by Moda Fabrics; Tuscany Silk batting from Hobbs Bonded Fibers; 50 wt. thread from Aurifil used to make sample. EQ8 was used to design this quilt.*

PROJECT NOTES

Read all instructions before beginning this project.

Stitch right sides together using a ¼" seam allowance unless otherwise specified.

Materials and cutting lists assume 40" of usable fabric width for yardage.

WOF – width of fabric
HST – half-square triangle
QST – quarter-square triangle

CUTTING

FROM ASSORTED RED PRINTS CUT A TOTAL OF:

- 80 (3½") A squares
- 160 (2" x 5") D rectangles
- 20 sets of 4 matching (2") B squares
- 12 (1½") F squares

FROM ASSORTED WHITE PRINTS CUT A TOTAL OF:

- 160 (2" x 5") D rectangles
- 80 (2" x 3½") C rectangles
- 420 (2") B squares

FROM WHITE PRINT CUT:

- 7 (2½" x WOF) strips, stitch short ends to short ends, then subcut into:
  2 (2½" x 72") G and 2 (2½" x 61½") H border strips
- 31 (1½" x 14") E rectangles

FROM RED PRINT CUT:

- 8 (2½" x WOF) binding strips

COMPLETING THE BLOCKS

1. Refer to Sew & Flip Corners on page 13 and use two white B squares and one red A square to make an A-B unit (Figure 1). Sew a white C rectangle to the left side and a white D rectangle to the bottom to complete an A-B-C-D unit. Make two and make two reverse A-B-C-D units.

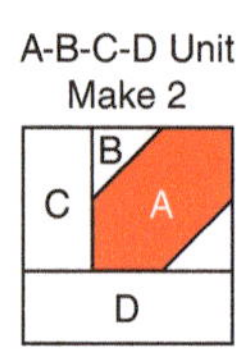

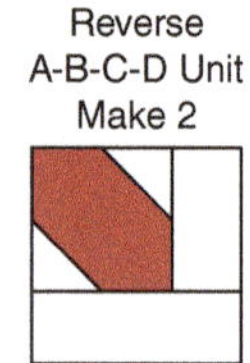

Figure 1

2. Using the Sew & Flip Corners method, sew a white B square to the top right corner of a red D rectangle to make a B-D unit (Figure 2). Repeat to make a reverse B-D unit. Sew both units and a white D rectangle together to make a B-D-D unit. Make four.

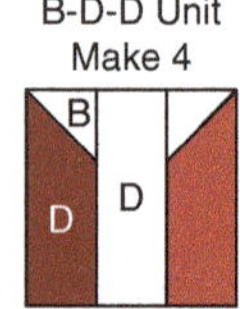

Figure 2

3. Sew four matching red B squares and five white B squares into three rows (Figure 3). Sew rows together to make a B-B unit.

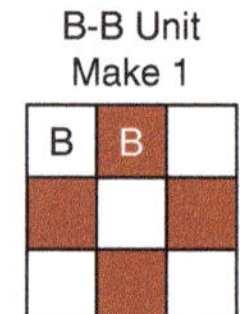

Figure 3

4. Lay out the units in three rows of three units each, noting the placement and orientation of the units (Figure 4). Sew the units into rows and join the rows to complete a block.

5. Repeat steps 1–4 to make 20 blocks.

Figure 4

COMPLETING THE QUILT

1. Join four blocks and three white E rectangles to make a pieced row. Make five.

2. Join four white E rectangles and three red F squares to make a sashing row. Make four.

3. Referring to the Assembly Diagram, lay out the pieced rows and sashing rows as shown. Join the rows to complete the quilt center. Press.

4. Sew the G and H border strips to the quilt top in alphabetical order.

5. Layer, baste, quilt as desired and bind referring to Quilting Basics. The photographed quilt was quilted with a swirl design. ●

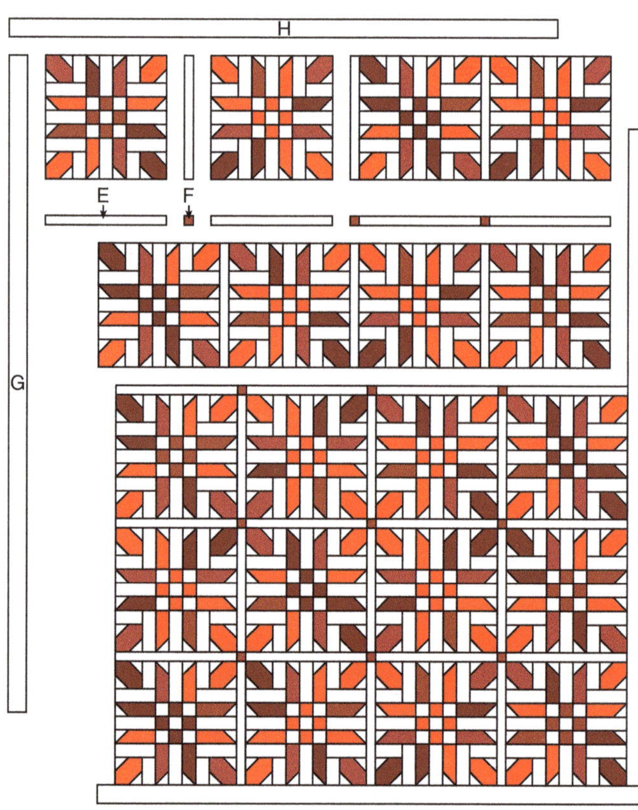

Who Drank the Fruit Punch?
Assembly Diagram 61" x 75"

WHO FOUND THE CATNIP?

Quilted by Darlene Szabo of Sew Graceful Quilting

This quilt is perfect for brightening up a cat lover's day.

SKILL LEVEL

Confident Beginner

FINISHED SIZES

Quilt Size: 48" x 54"
Block Size: 12" x 10"
Number of Blocks: 12

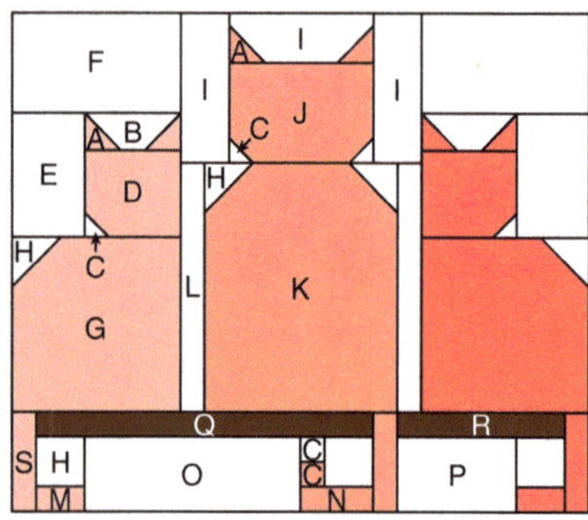

Cat Trio
12" x 10" Finished Block
Make 12

MATERIALS

- 2⅛ yards white solid*
- 1¼ yards assorted prints*
- ⅜ yard assorted black prints*
- ¼ yard brown print*
- ¾ yard floral print*
- ⅝ yard blue print*
- 4 yards backing*
- 56" x 62" batting*
- Thread*
- Basic sewing tools and supplies

**Scrap fabrics from various collections by Moda Fabrics; Tuscany Silk batting from Hobbs Bonded Fibers; 50 wt. thread from Aurifil used to make sample. EQ8 was used to design this quilt.*

PROJECT NOTES

Read all instructions before beginning this project.

Stitch right sides together using a ¼" seam allowance unless otherwise specified.

Materials and cutting lists assume 40" of usable fabric width for yardage.

WOF – width of fabric
HST – half-square triangle ⧄
QST – quarter-square triangle ⊠

CUTTING

FROM WHITE SOLID CUT:

- 5 (2½" x WOF) strips, stitch short ends to short ends, then subcut into:
  2 (2½" x 46½") V and 2 (2½" x 44½") W border strips
- 4 (2½" x WOF) strips, stitch short ends to short ends, then subcut into:
  3 (2½" x 40½") U strips
- 8 (2½" x 10½") T rectangles
- 24 (2½" x 4") F rectangles
- 12 (2" x 5") O rectangles
- 12 (2" x 3") P rectangles
- 24 (2" x 3") E rectangles
- 36 (1½" x 3½") I rectangles
- 84 (1½") H squares
- 24 (1¼" x 2½") B rectangles
- 24 (1" x 5½") L rectangles
- 48 (1") C squares

Inspiration

"This design was inspired by the cat islands of Japan."
—Wendy Sheppard

FROM ASSORTED PRINTS CUT A TOTAL OF:

- 20 matching sets of:
  - 1 (4") G square
  - 1 (2¼" x 2½") D rectangle
  - 2 (1¼") A squares
  - 1 (1" x 2½") S rectangle
  - 1 (1" x 1½") M rectangle
- 12 matching sets of:
  - 1 (4½" x 5½") K rectangle
  - 1 (2½" x 3½") J rectangle
  - 2 (1¼") A squares
  - 1 (1" x 2½") S rectangle
  - 1 (1" x 2") N rectangle
  - 1 (1") C square

FROM ASSORTED BLACK PRINTS CUT A TOTAL OF:

- 4 matching sets of:
  - 1 (4") G square
  - 1 (2¼" x 2½") D rectangle
  - 2 (1¼") A squares
  - 1 (1" x 2½") S rectangle
  - 1 (1" x 1½") M rectangle

FROM BROWN PRINT CUT:

- 12 (1" x 7½") Q rectangles
- 12 (1" x 4") R rectangles

FROM FLORAL PRINT CUT:

- 5 (2½" x WOF) strips, stitch short ends to short ends, then subcut into:
  - 2 (2½" x 50½") X and 2 (2½" x 48½") Y border strips

FROM BLUE PRINT CUT:

- 6 (2½" x WOF) binding strips

COMPLETING THE BLOCKS

Note: *For steps 1–3, use one set of matching assorted prints.*

1. Refer to Sew & Flip Corners on page 13 and use two assorted print A squares and a white B rectangle to make an A-B unit (Figure 1).

A-B Unit
Make 1

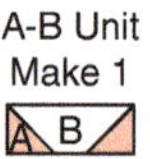

Figure 1

2. In the same way, sew a white C square to the bottom left corner of an assorted print D rectangle to make a C-D unit (Figure 2). Sew the C-D unit to the bottom of the A-B unit. Sew a white E rectangle to the left side and a white F rectangle to the top to make a C-D-E-F unit.

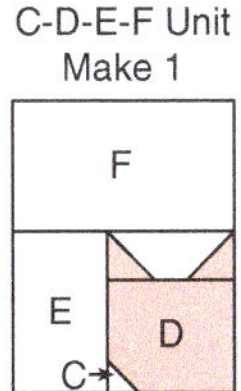

Figure 2

3. Using the sew-and-flip method, sew a white H square to the top left corner of an assorted print G rectangle to make a G-H unit (Figure 3). Sew the G-H unit to the bottom of the C-D-E-F unit to make a cat 1 unit. Use another set of matching assorted prints to make a reverse cat 1 unit.

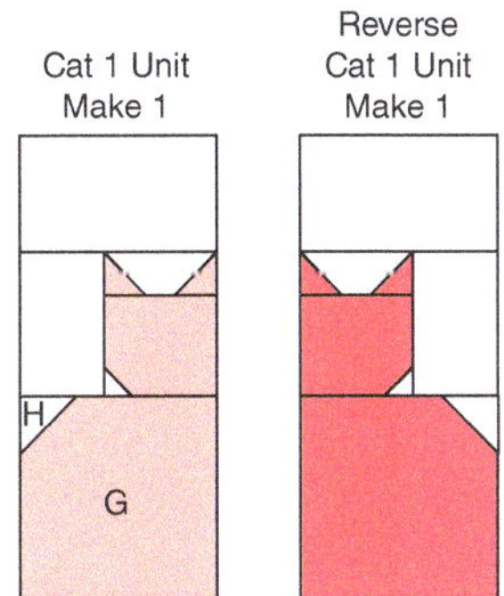

Figure 3

Note: *For steps 4–6, use one set of matching assorted prints.*

4. Using the sew-and-flip method, sew two assorted print A squares to the bottom corners of a white I rectangle to make an A-I unit (Figure 4).

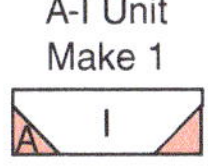

Figure 4

5. In the same way, sew two white C squares to the bottom of an assorted print J rectangle to make a C-J unit (Figure 5). Sew the A-I unit to top of the C-J unit. Sew two white I rectangles to the sides to complete a C-J-I unit.

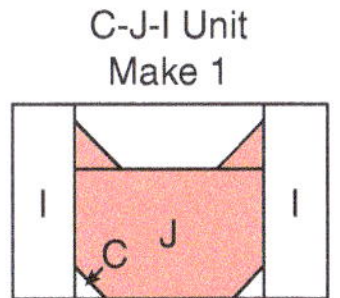

Figure 5

6. Using the sew-and-flip method, sew two white H squares to the top corners of an assorted print K rectangle to make an H-K unit (Figure 6). Sew two white L rectangles to the sides to make a H-K-L unit. Sew the C-J-I unit to top of the H-K-L unit to make a cat 2 unit.

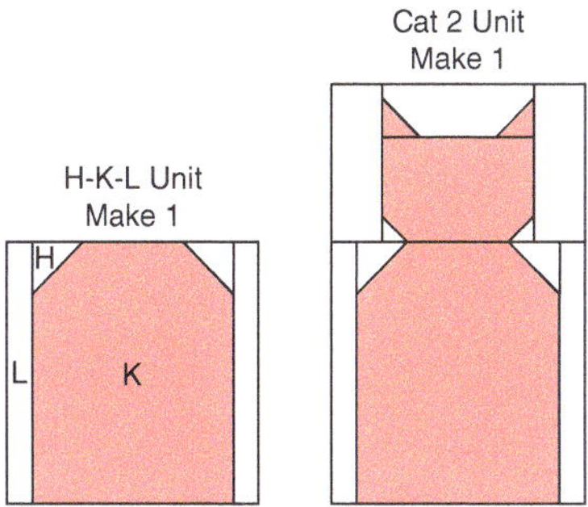

Figure 6

7. Sew the cat 1 unit and the reverse cat 1 unit to either side of the cat 2 unit to make a cat trio unit (Figure 7).

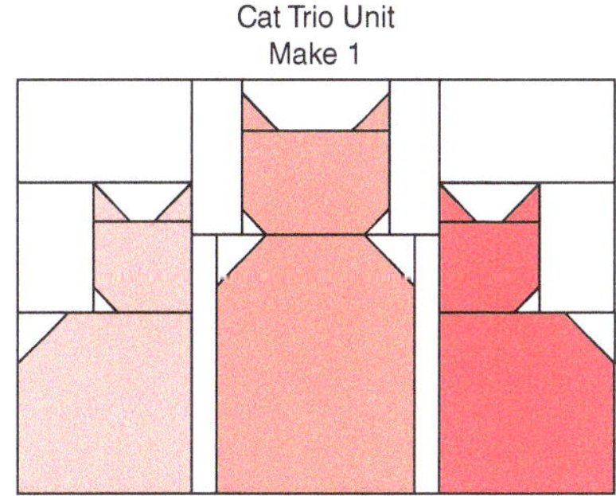

Figure 7

8. Sew an assorted print M rectangle to the bottom of a white H square to make an H-M unit (Figure 8). Make two.

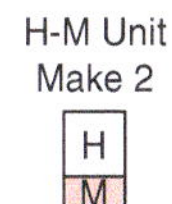

Figure 8

9. Sew together one assorted print C square and one white C square to make a C-C unit (Figure 9). Sew a white H rectangle to the right side of the C-C unit and then sew an assorted print N rectangle to the bottom to make a C-H-N unit.

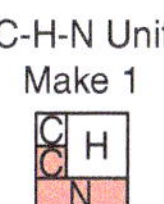

Figure 9

10. Sew an H-M unit to the left side of a white O rectangle (Figure 10). Sew the C-H-N unit to the right end of the O rectangle. Sew a brown Q rectangle to the top to make an O-Q unit.

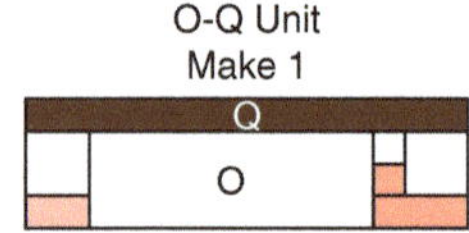

Figure 10

11. Sew an H-M unit to the right side of a white P rectangle and then sew a brown R rectangle to the top to make a P-R unit (Figure 11).

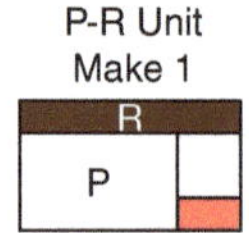

Figure 11

12. Lay out the O-Q and P-R units, alternating with matching S rectangles, then sew together to make a cat tails unit (Figure 12).

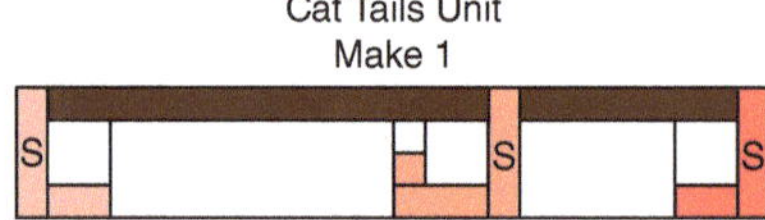

Figure 12

13. Sew the cat trio unit to the top of the cat tails unit to complete a Cat Trio block (Figure 13).

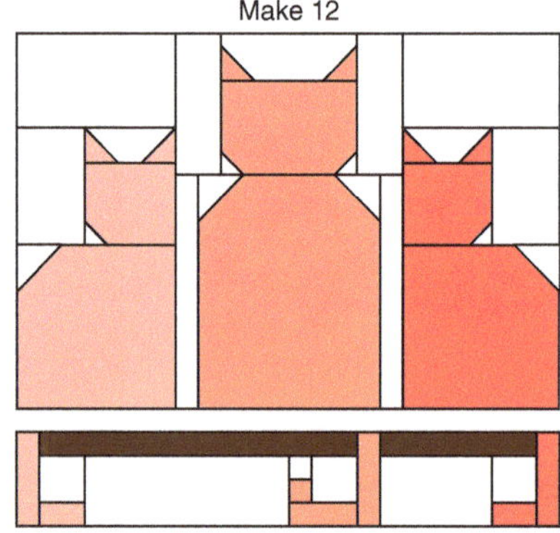

Figure 13

14. Repeat steps 1–13 to make 12 Cat Trio blocks.

COMPLETING THE QUILT

1. Referring to the Assembly Diagram, lay out the blocks, white T rectangles and white U strips in seven rows.

2. Sew into rows and join the rows to complete the quilt center. Press.

3. Sew the V–Y border strips to the quilt top in alphabetical order.

4. Layer, baste, quilt as desired and bind referring to Quilting Basics. The photographed quilt was quilted with a floral design. ●

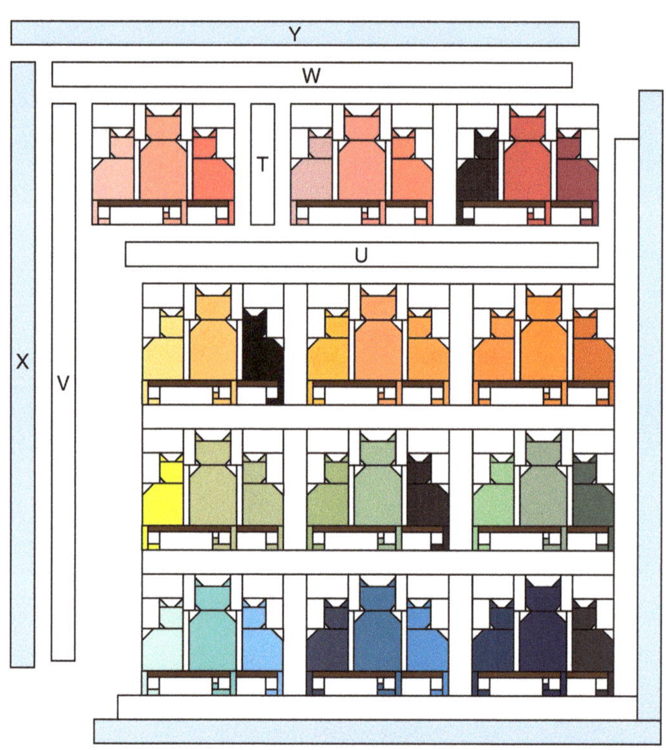

Who Found the Catnip?
Assembly Diagram 48" x 54"

WHOSE BROAD STRIPES & BRIGHT STARS?

Quilted by Darlene Szabo of Sew Graceful Quilting

These sparkling blocks go together so quickly!

SKILL LEVEL

Confident Beginner

FINISHED SIZES

Quilt Size: 68" x 68"
Block Size: 12" x 12"
Number of Blocks: 25

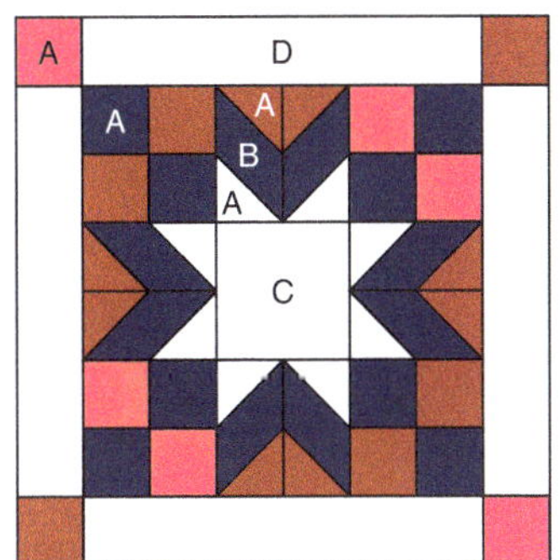

Framed Star
12" x 12" Finished Block
Make 25

MATERIALS

- 1¼ yards total assorted red prints*
- 2¾ yards total assorted white prints*
- 2½ yards total assorted navy prints*
- ⅝ yard total assorted pink prints*
- 1¼ yards blue print*
- ⅔ yard red print*
- 4½ yards backing*
- 76" x 76" batting*
- Thread*
- Basic sewing tools and supplies

**Scrap fabrics from various collections by Moda Fabrics; Tuscany Silk batting from Hobbs Bonded Fibers; 50 wt. thread from Aurifil used to make sample. EQ8 was used to design this quilt.*

PROJECT NOTES

Read all instructions before beginning this project.

Stitch right sides together using a ¼" seam allowance unless otherwise specified.

Materials and cutting lists assume 40" of usable fabric width for yardage.

Arrows indicate directions to press seams.

WOF – width of fabric
HST – half-square triangle ⧅
QST – quarter-square triangle ⊠

Inspiration

"Seeing the sea of flags at various patriotic events was the starting point for this design. I would not complain if I were to make only these blocks for the rest of my life!" —Wendy Sheppard

CUTTING

FROM ASSORTED RED PRINTS CUT:

- 350 (2") A squares

FROM ASSORTED WHITE PRINTS CUT:

- 25 sets of 1 (3½") C square and 8 (2") A squares
- 100 (2" x 9½") D rectangles
- 16 (1½") F squares

FROM ASSORTED NAVY PRINTS CUT:

- 25 sets of 8 (2" x 3½") B rectangles and 8 (2") A squares

FROM ASSORTED PINK PRINTS CUT:

- 150 (2") A squares

FROM BLUE PRINT CUT:

- 40 (1½" x 12½") E strips
- 7 (2½" x WOF) strips, stitch short ends to short ends, then subcut into:
  2 (2½" x 64½") G and 2 (2½" x 68½") H border strips

FROM RED PRINT CUT:

- 8 (2½" x WOF) binding strips

COMPLETING THE BLOCKS

1. Each block includes 14 assorted red A squares, one set of matching white pieces (one C square and eight A squares), one set of matching navy pieces (eight B rectangles and eight A squares), six assorted pink A squares and four assorted white D rectangles. Select pieces for one block.

2. Refer to Sew & Flip Corners and add an assorted red and a white A square to each navy B rectangle (Figure 1). Make four A-B-A units of each orientation.

A-B-A Units
Make 4 each per block

Figure 1

3. Join one A-B-A unit of each orientation to make a star point unit measuring 3½" square from raw edge to raw edge (Figure 2). Make four star point units.

Star Point Unit
Make 4 per block

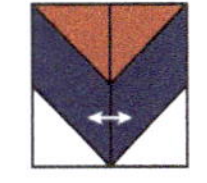

Figure 2

4. Use two navy and two assorted red A squares to arrange and sew two rows of two squares each (Figure 3). Join the rows to make a red four-patch unit measuring 3½" square. Make two. In the same way, use two navy and two assorted pink A squares to make a pink four-patch unit. Make two.

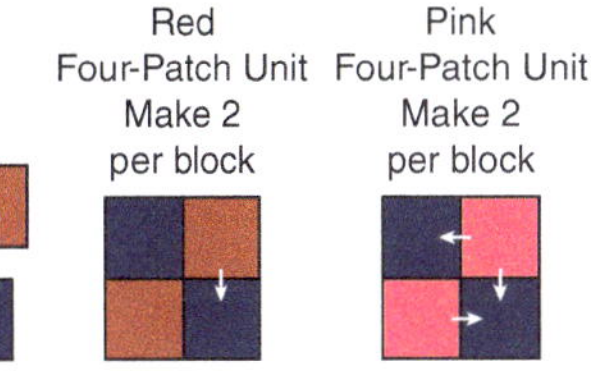

Figure 3

SEW & FLIP CORNERS

Use this method to add triangle corners in a quilt block.

1. Draw a diagonal line from corner to corner on the wrong side of the specified square. Place the square, right sides together, on the indicated corner of the larger piece, making sure the line is oriented in the correct direction indicated by the pattern (Figure 1).

2. Sew on the drawn line. Trim ¼" away from sewn line (Figure 2).

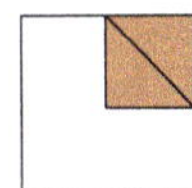

Figure 1

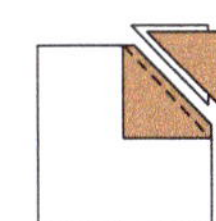

Figure 2

3. Open and press to reveal the corner triangle (Figure 3).

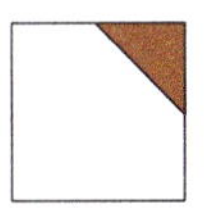

Figure 3

4. If desired, square up the finished unit to the required unfinished size.

5. Arrange and sew three rows using two red four-patch units, four star point units, two pink four-patch units and the matching C square (Figure 4). Join the rows to complete a star measuring 9½" square.

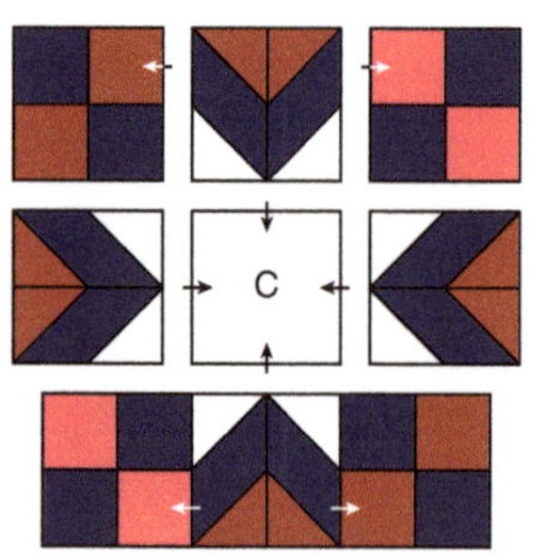

Figure 4

6. Arrange and sew three rows using two assorted pink A squares, four assorted D rectangles, two assorted red A squares and a star (Figure 5). Join the rows to complete a Framed Star block.

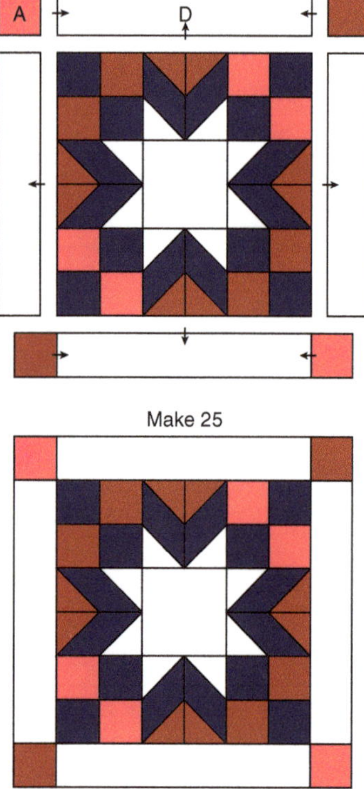

Figure 5

7. Repeat steps 1–6 to make 25 total Framed Star blocks.

COMPLETING THE QUILT

1. Referring to the Assembly Diagram, lay out the blocks in five rows of five each. Add E strips and F squares between the blocks as shown.

2. Sew five block rows of five blocks and four E strips each. Sew four sashing rows of five E strips and four F squares each. Join the rows, alternating block and sashing rows, to complete the quilt center. Press.

3. Sew the G and H border strips to the quilt top in alphabetical order.

4. Layer, baste, quilt as desired and bind referring to Quilting Basics. The photographed quilt was quilted with an edge-to-edge swirl design. ●

Here's a Tip

Try an even scrappier version of this design by using pieces cut from a variety of white and navy fabrics in each block, instead of the matching sets called for in the instructions. This way you can incorporate smaller pieces of fabric from your stash.

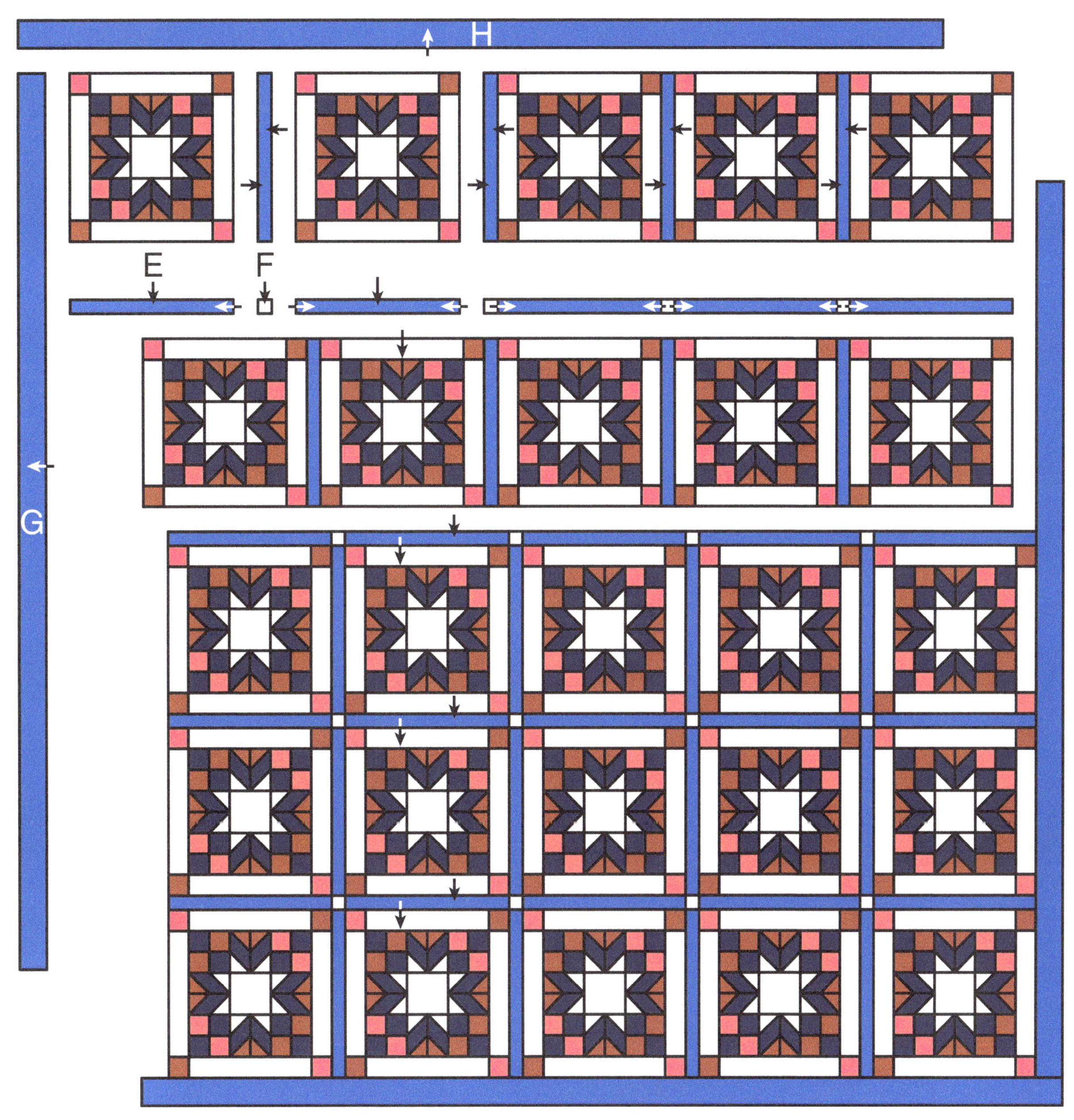

Whose Broad Stripes & Bright Stars?
Assembly Diagram 68" x 68"

Inspiration

"Snowball blocks were the starting point for this design. I wanted to see how combining a group of them would look." —Wendy Sheppard

WHO LOST THEIR MARBLES?

Quilted by Darlene Szabo of Sew Graceful Quilting

This design is perfect for using up fabrics of a similar theme in your collection.

SKILL LEVEL

Confident Beginner

FINISHED SIZES

Quilt Size: 54" x 64"

Block Size: 9" x 9"

Number of Blocks: 30

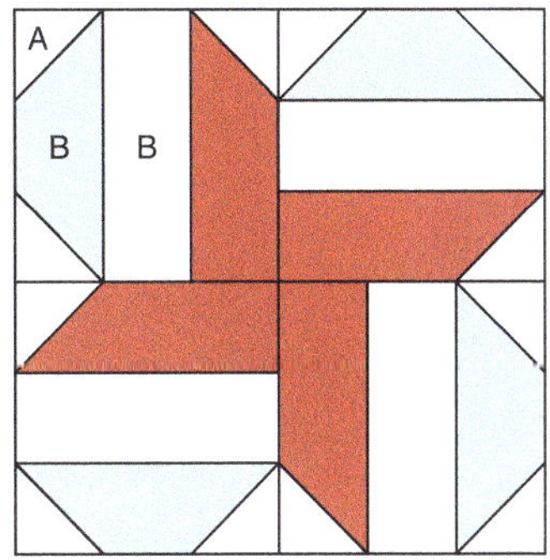

Marbles
9" x 9" Finished Block
Make 30

MATERIALS

- 3⅛ yards ivory solid*
- 2 yards assorted prints*
- ⅝ yard gray print*
- 3¾ yards backing*
- 62" x 72" batting*
- Thread*
- Basic sewing tools and supplies

**Scrap fabrics from various collections by Moda Fabrics; Tuscany Silk batting from Hobbs Bonded Fibers; 50 wt. thread from Aurifil used to make sample. EQ8 was used to design this quilt.*

PROJECT NOTES

Read all instructions before beginning this project.

Stitch right sides together using a ¼" seam allowance unless otherwise specified.

Materials and cutting lists assume 40" of usable fabric width for yardage.

Arrows indicate directions to press seams.

WOF – width of fabric
HST – half-square triangle
QST – quarter-square triangle

CUTTING

FROM IVORY SOLID CUT:

- 120 (2" x 5") B rectangles
- 360 (2") A squares
- 49 (1½" x 9½") C strips
- 6 (3" x WOF) strips, stitch short ends to short ends, then subcut into:
  2 (3" x 59½") E and 2 (3" x 54½") F border strips

FROM ASSORTED PRINTS CUT:

- 60 sets of 4 matching (2" x 5") B rectangles
- 1 set of 20 matching (1½") D squares

FROM GRAY PRINT CUT:

- 7 (2½" x WOF) binding strips

COMPLETING THE BLOCKS

1. Each block includes two contrasting sets of four print B rectangles, plus 12 ivory A squares and four ivory B rectangles. Select pieces for one block.

2. Refer to Sew & Flip Corners on page 13 and add two A squares to each of four matching B rectangles to make four edge units (Figure 1a). In the same way, add one A square to each of the four remaining print B rectangles to make four center units (Figure 1b).

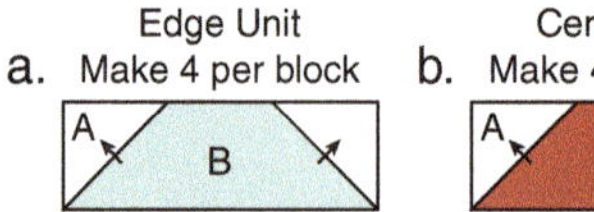

Figure 1

3. Join one edge unit, one ivory B rectangle and one center unit to make a quarter-block (Figure 2). Make four quarter-blocks.

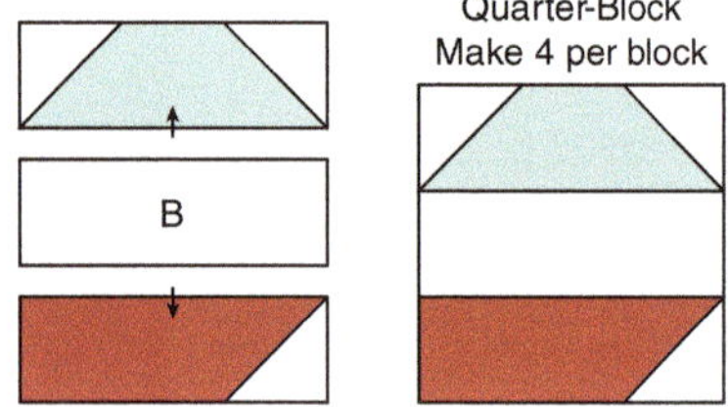

Figure 2

4. Arrange and sew two rows of two quarter-blocks each, watching orientation (Figure 3). Join the rows to complete a Marbles block.

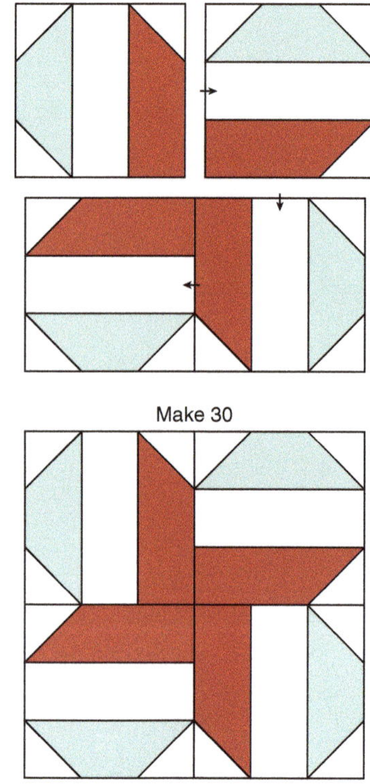

Figure 3

5. Repeat steps 1–4 to make 30 Marbles blocks total.

COMPLETING THE QUILT

1. Referring to the Assembly Diagram, lay out the blocks in six rows of five blocks each. Add C strips and D squares between the blocks as shown.

2. Sew six block rows of five blocks and four C strips each. Sew five sashing rows of five C strips and four D squares each. Join the block and sashing rows, alternating, to complete the quilt center. Press.

3. Sew the E and F border strips to the quilt top in alphabetical order.

4. Layer, baste, quilt as desired and bind referring to Quilting Basics. The photographed quilt was quilted with an edge-to-edge swirl design. ●

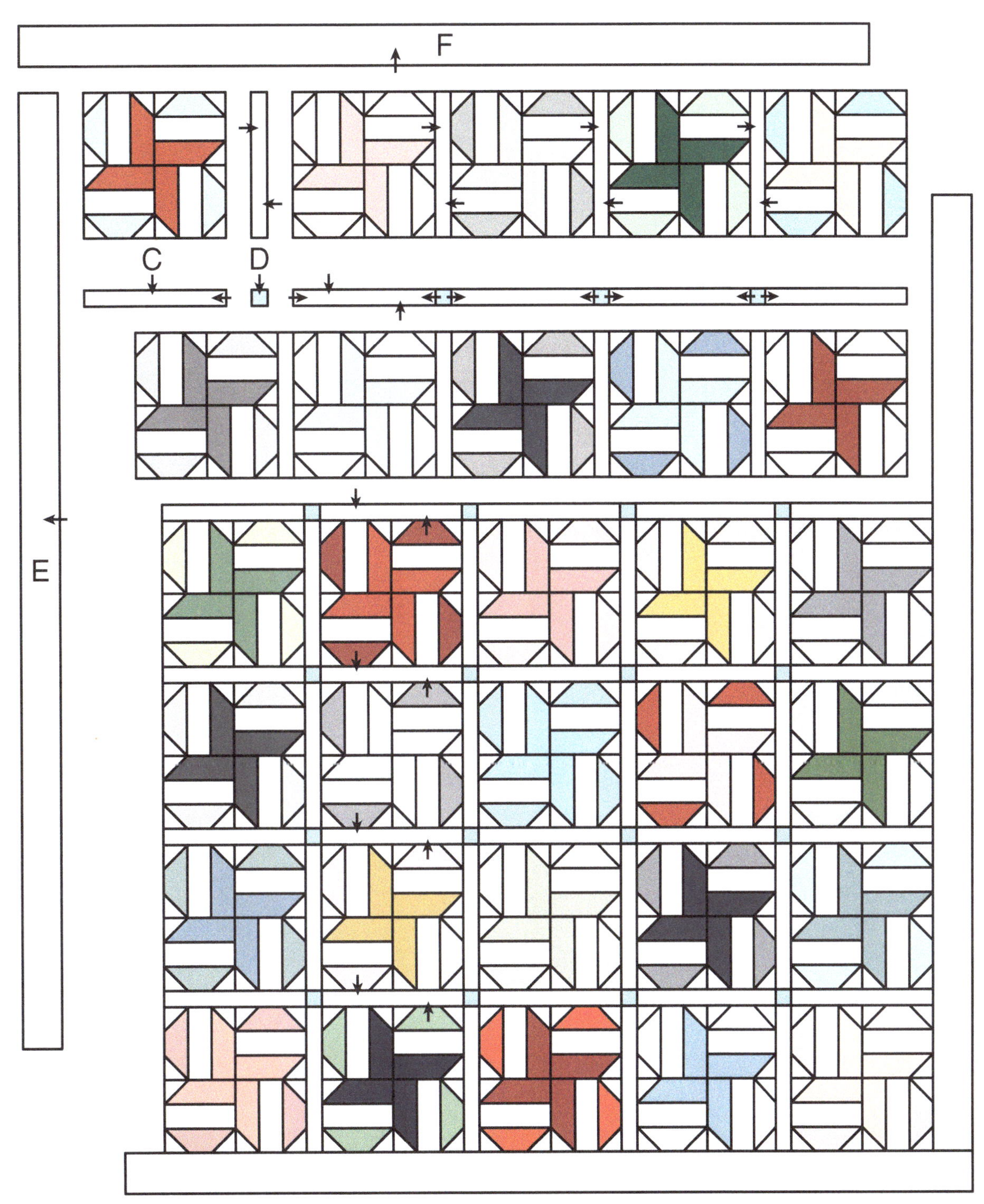

Who Lost Their Marbles?
Assembly Diagram 54" x 64"

Inspiration

"I have always loved Basket quilt blocks. I am always thinking about different Basket blocks to make!" —Wendy Sheppard

WHO TIPPED THE BASKET?

Quilted by Darlene Szabo of Sew Graceful Quilting

These cute Basket blocks are so fun to make you may have trouble stopping at just 25 of them!

SKILL LEVEL

Confident Beginner

FINISHED SIZES

Quilt Size: 46" x 46"

Block Size: 6" x 6"

Number of Blocks: 49

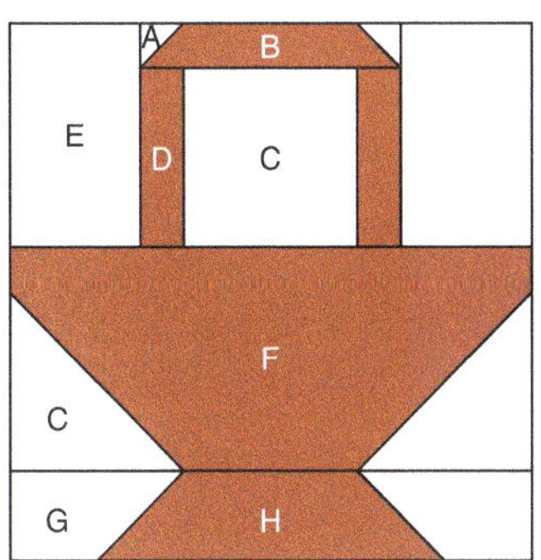

Basket
6" x 6" Finished Block
Make 25

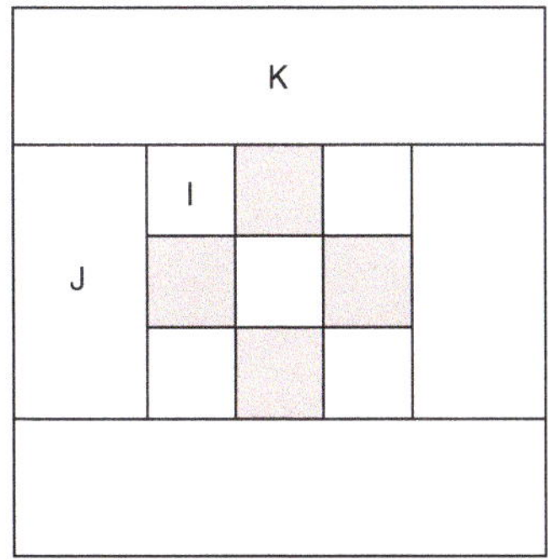

Framed Nine-Patch
6" x 6" Finished Block
Make 24

MATERIALS

- 2½ yards ivory solid*
- 1¼ yards assorted prints*
- ⅔ yard tan print*
- 3⅛ yards backing*
- 54" x 54" batting*
- Thread*
- Basic sewing tools and supplies

**Scrap fabrics from various collections by Moda Fabrics; Tuscany Silk batting from Hobbs Bonded Fibers; 50 wt. thread from Aurifil used to make sample. EQ8 was used to design this quilt.*

PROJECT NOTES

Read all instructions before beginning this project.

Stitch right sides together using a ¼" seam allowance unless otherwise specified.

Materials and cutting lists assume 40" of usable fabric width for yardage.

Arrows indicate directions to press seams.

WOF – width of fabric
HST – half-square triangle ⧄
QST – quarter-square triangle ⊠

Here's a Tip

When searching your scrap bin for assorted prints, keep in mind that all the print pieces needed for a Basket block can be cut from a 7" square of fabric.

CUTTING

FROM IVORY SOLID CUT:

- 75 (2½") C squares
- 48 (2" x 6½") K rectangles
- 48 (2" x 3½") J rectangles
- 50 (2" x 3") E rectangles
- 5 (1½" x WOF) I strips
- 50 (1½" x 2½") G rectangles
- 50 (1") A squares
- 5 (2½" x WOF) strips, stitch short ends to short ends, then subcut into:
  2 (2½" x 42½") L and 2 (2½" x 46½") M border strips

FROM ASSORTED PRINTS CUT 25 SETS OF:

- 1 (3" x 6½") F rectangle
- 1 (1½" x 4½") H rectangle
- 1 (1" x 3½") B rectangle
- 2 (1" x 2½") D rectangles

FROM TAN PRINT CUT:

- 4 (1½" x WOF) I strips
- 6 (2½" x WOF) binding strips

COMPLETING THE BLOCKS

1. Each Basket block includes one set of matching print pieces (one each of the F, H and B rectangles, and two D rectangles) plus two A squares, three C squares, two E rectangles and two G rectangles of the ivory solid. Select pieces for one block.

2. Refer to Sew & Flip Corners on page 13 and add two A squares to the B rectangle as shown (Figure 1).

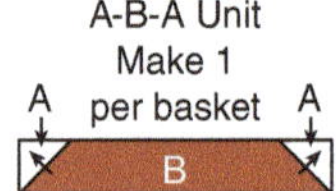

Figure 1

3. In the same way, add two C squares to the F rectangle (Figure 2).

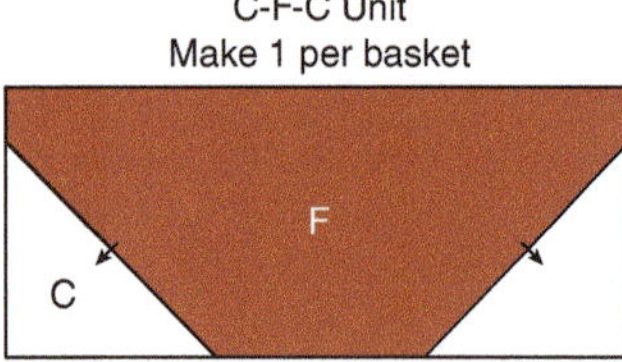

Figure 2

4. Using the same sew-and-flip technique, add two G rectangles to the H rectangle (Figure 3).

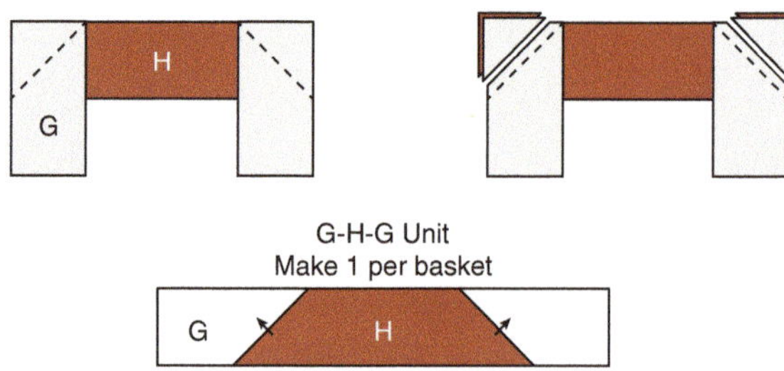

Figure 3

5. Sew D rectangles to opposite sides of the remaining C square (Figure 4). Sew the A-B-A unit to the top to complete the handle, measuring 3" x 3½" from raw edge to raw edge.

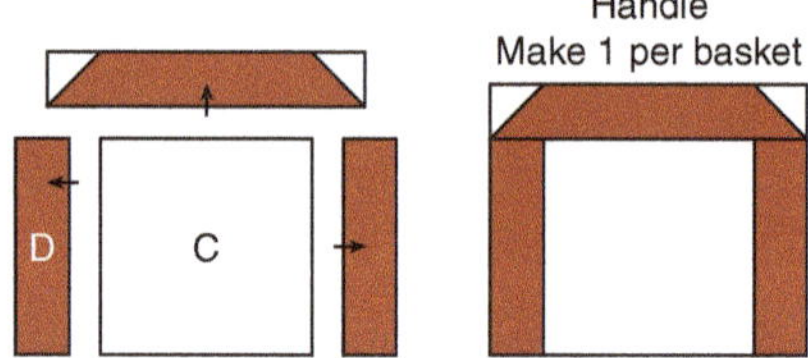

Figure 4

6. Add E rectangles to opposite sides of the handle (Figure 5). Join the handle row, C-F-C unit and G-H-G unit to complete a Basket block.

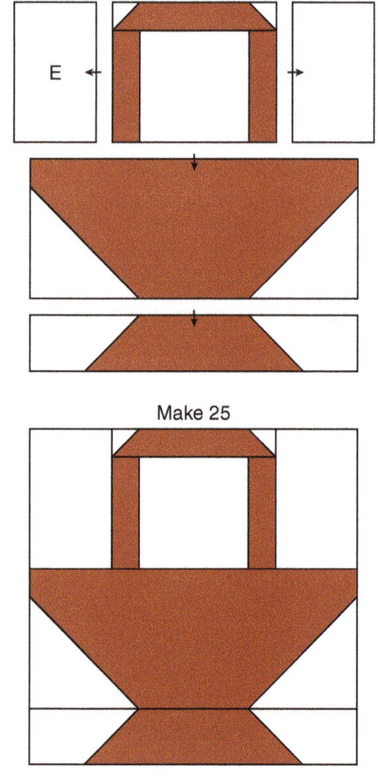

Figure 5

7. Repeat steps 1–6 to make 25 Basket blocks total.

8. Sew two ivory I strips to a tan I strip to make an ivory-tan-ivory strip set (Figure 6). Make two. From the strip sets, cut 48 segments each 1½" wide.

Sew two tan I strips to an ivory I strip to make a tan-ivory-tan strip set. From the strip set, cut 24 segments each 1½" wide.

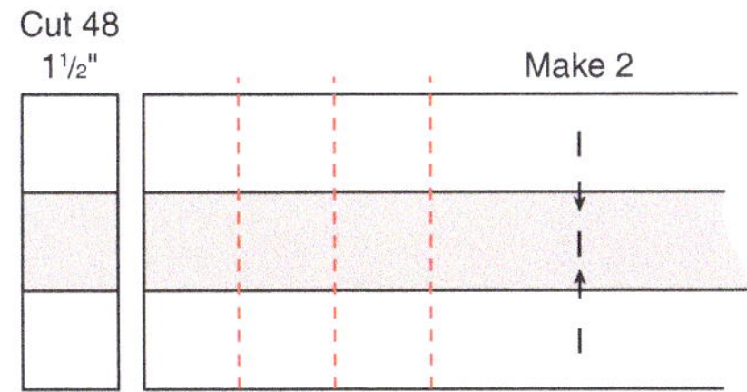

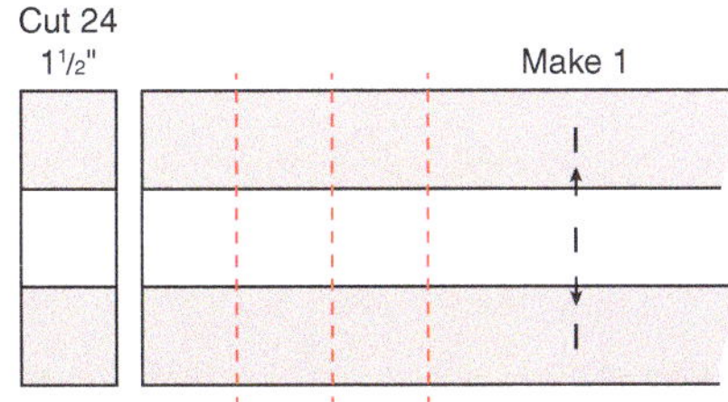

Figure 6

9. Sew two ivory-tan-ivory segments to a tan-ivory-tan segment to make a nine-patch unit measuring 3½" square. (Figure 7). Make 24.

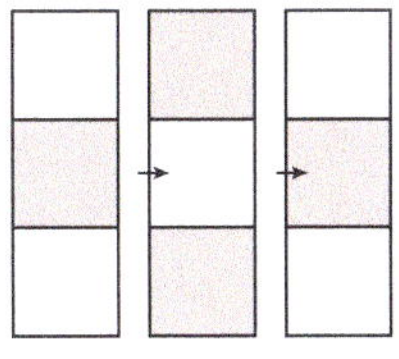

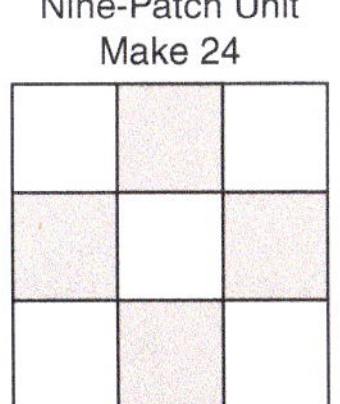

Figure 7

10. Sew J rectangles to opposite sides of a nine-patch unit (Figure 8). Add K rectangles to the top and bottom to complete a Framed Nine-Patch block. Make 24.

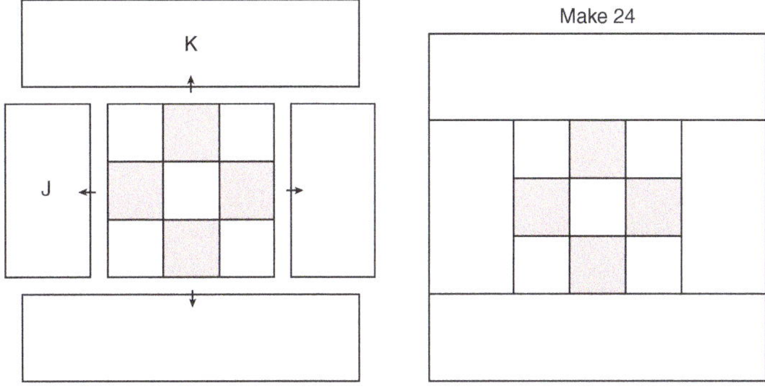

Figure 8

COMPLETING THE QUILT

1. Referring to the Assembly Diagram, lay out the blocks in seven rows of seven blocks each, alternating Basket and Framed Nine-Patch blocks.

2. Sew the blocks into rows and join the rows to complete the quilt center. Press.

3. Sew the L and M border strips to the quilt top in alphabetical order.

4. Layer, baste, quilt as desired and bind referring to Quilting Basics. The photographed quilt was quilted with an edge-to-edge fan design. ●

Who Tipped the Basket?
Assembly Diagram 46" x 46"

Inspiration

"My love of blue transferware inspired this fresh blue design." —Wendy Sheppard

WHO TENDS THE GARDEN?

Quilted by Darlene Szabo of Sew Graceful Quilting

The Shoofly blocks in this quilt are perfect as leaders and enders as you work on other quilt projects. When you have made enough, sewing up the quilt center will be a cinch.

SKILL LEVEL

Confident Beginner

FINISHED SIZES

Quilt Size: 70" x 79"

Block Size: 4½" x 4½" and 9" x 15"

Number of Blocks: 80 and 18

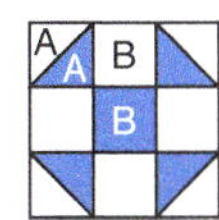

Shoofly
4½" x 4½" Block
Make 80

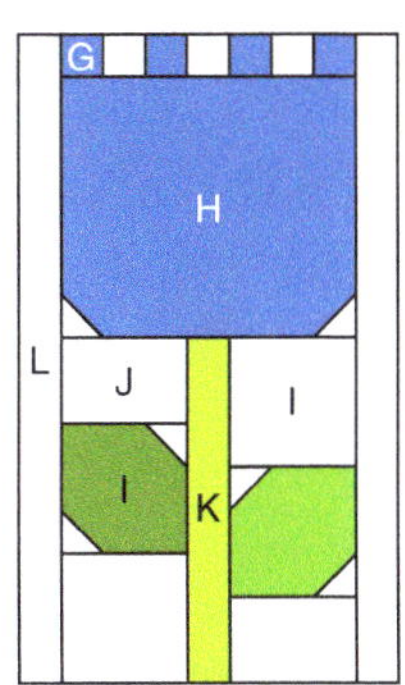

Flower
9" x 15" Finished Block
Make 18

MATERIALS

- 1 yard total assorted green prints*
- 2½ yards total assorted blue prints*
- 5 yards total assorted low-volume prints*
- ¾ yard binding fabric*
- 4⅞ yards backing fabric*
- 78" x 87" batting*
- Thread*
- Basic sewing tools and supplies

**Scrap fabrics from various collections by Moda Fabrics; Tuscany Silk batting from Hobbs Bonded Fibers; 50 wt. thread from Aurifil used to make sample. EQ8 was used to design this quilt.*

PROJECT NOTES

Read all instructions before beginning this project.

Stitch right sides together using a ¼" seam allowance unless otherwise specified.

Arrows indicate directions to press seams.

Materials and cutting lists assume 40" of usable fabric width for yardage.

WOF – width of fabric
HST – half-square triangle ⧅
QST – quarter-square triangle ⊠

CUTTING

FROM ASSORTED GREEN PRINTS CUT:

- 36 (3½") I squares
- 24 (2½") A squares
- 12 (2") B squares
- 18 (1½" x 8½") K rectangles

FROM ASSORTED BLUE PRINTS CUT:

- 18 sets of 1 (6½" x 7½") H rectangle and 4 (1½") G squares
- 80 sets of 2 (2½") A squares and 1 (2") B square

FROM ASSORTED LOW-VOLUME PRINTS CUT:

- 8 (5" x 9½") C rectangles
- 8 (5") D squares
- 36 (3½") I squares
- 8 (2½" x WOF) strips, sew short ends to short ends, then subcut into:
  2 (2½" x 75½") M strips and 2 (2½" x 70½") N strips
- 36 (2½" x 3½") J rectangles
- 184 (2½") A squares
- 368 (2") B squares
- 36 (1½" x 15½") L rectangles
- 216 (1½") G squares
- 8 (1¼" x 15½") F rectangles
- 8 (1¼" x 14") E rectangles

FROM BINDING FABRIC CUT:

- 8 (2½" x WOF) binding strips

COMPLETING THE BLOCKS

1. Referring to Half-Square Triangles, use one each blue and low-volume A squares to make blue HST units (Figure 1). Trim to 2". Make a total of 320. In the same way, make a total of 48 green HST units.

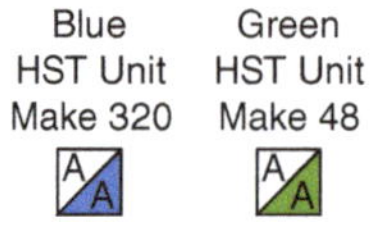

Blue HST Unit Make 320 | Green HST Unit Make 48

Figure 1

2. Lay out four blue HST units, one blue B square and four low-volume B squares into three rows of three (Figure 2). Sew into rows and join the rows to make one blue Shoofly block. Make 80. In the same way, make 12 green Shoofly blocks.

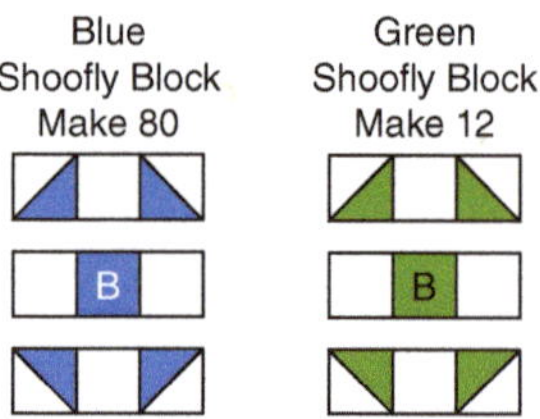

Figure 2

3. Lay out three green Shoofly blocks, two C rectangles and two D squares into three rows of three (Figure 3). Sew into rows and join the rows to make one corner unit. Make four.

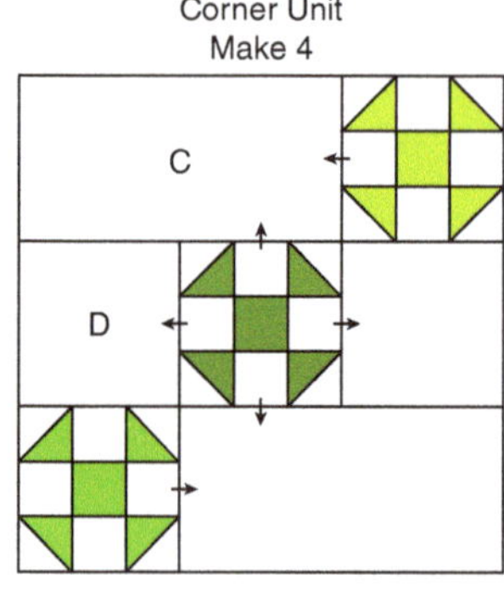

Figure 3

HALF-SQUARE TRIANGLES

Half-square triangles (HSTs) are a basic unit of quilting used in many blocks or on their own. This construction method will yield two HSTs.

1. Refer to the pattern for size to cut squares. The standard formula is to add ⅞" to the finished size of the square. Cut two squares from different colors this size. For example, for a 3" finished HST unit, cut 3⅞" squares.

2. Draw a diagonal line from corner to corner on the wrong side of the lightest color square. Layer the squares right sides together. Stitch ¼" on either side of the drawn line (Figure A).

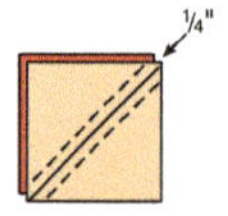

Figure A

3. Cut the squares apart on the drawn line, leaving a ¼" seam allowance and making two HST units referring to Figure B.

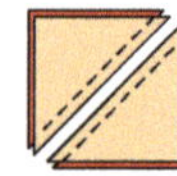

Figure B

4. Open the HST units and press seam allowances toward the darker fabric making two HST units (Figure C). ●

Figure C

4. Sew E rectangles to opposite sides of one corner unit. Sew F rectangles to the top and bottom (Figure 4). Make four framed corner units.

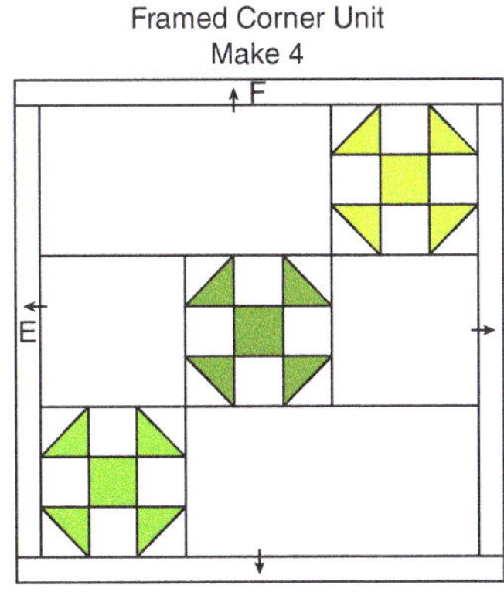

Figure 4

5. Sew together four blue G squares alternating with three low-volume G squares into a row. Sew one H rectangle to the bottom and then, referring to Sew & Flip Corners on page 13, add G squares to the bottom corners to complete a flower unit (Figure 5).

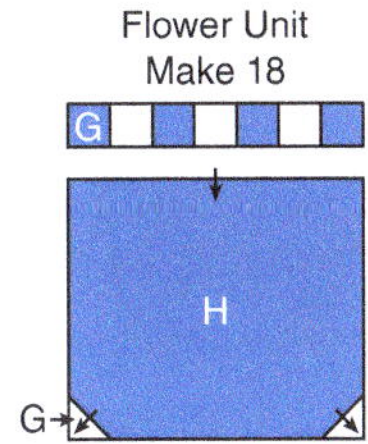

Figure 5

6. Refer to Sew & Flip Corners on page 13 and add G squares to opposite corners of one green I square to make a leaf unit (Figure 6). Make 36.

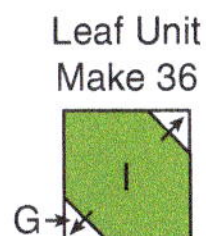

Figure 6

7. Lay out two leaf units, two I squares, two J rectangles and one K rectangle into three rows. Sew into rows and join the rows to make one leaf/stem unit (Figure 7). Make 18.

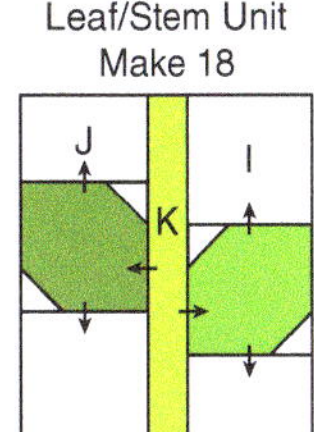

Figure 7

8. Sew one flower unit to the top of one leaf/stem unit and then add L rectangles to opposite sides (Figure 8). Make 18.

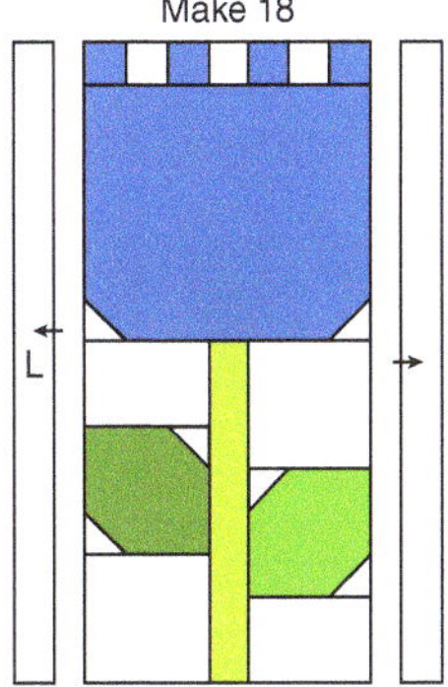

Figure 8

COMPLETING THE QUILT

1. Lay out the blue Shoofly blocks into 10 rows of eight blocks each. Sew the blocks into rows and join the rows to make the quilt center.

2. Sew together five flower blocks to make a side border. Make two. Sew to opposite sides of the quilt center. Sew together four flower blocks and two framed corner units into the top row. Repeat for the bottom row. Sew to the top and bottom of the quilt.

3. Sew M strips to opposite long sides of the quilt center and N strips to the top and bottom to complete the quilt top.

4. Layer, baste, quilt as desired and bind referring to Quilting Basics. The photographed quilt was quilted with an overall swirl design. ●

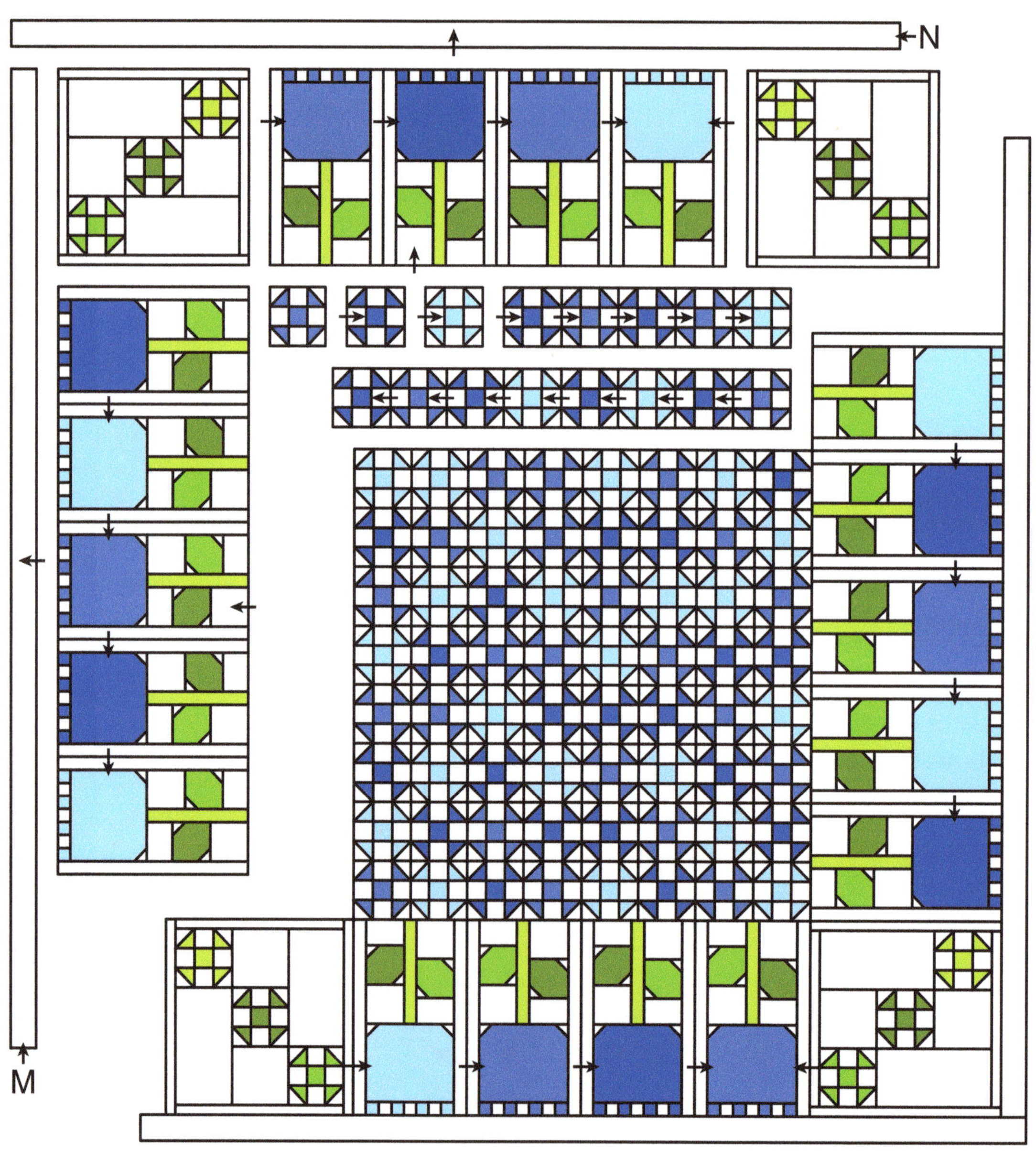

Who Tends the Garden?
Assembly Diagram 70" x 79"

WHO'S SNAILING AROUND TOWN?

Quilted by Darlene Szabo of Sew Graceful Quilting

These easy snail house blocks in a rainbow palette make a cheerful and happy quilt!

SKILL LEVEL

Confident Beginner

FINISHED SIZES

Quilt Size: 68" x 69"

Block Size: 12" x 12" and 5" x 12"

Number of Blocks: 12 and 16

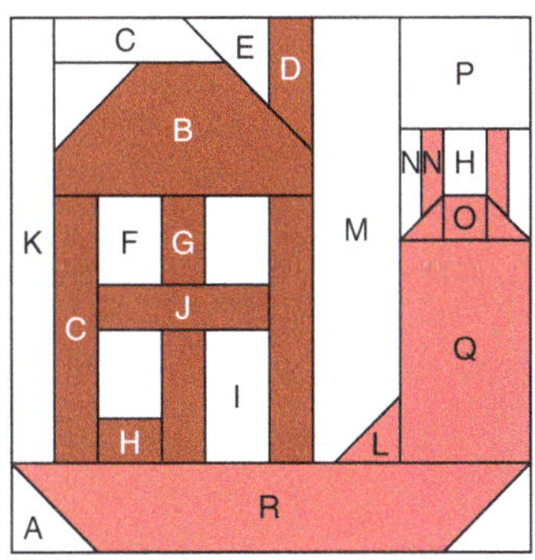

Snail
12" x 12" Finished Block
Make 12

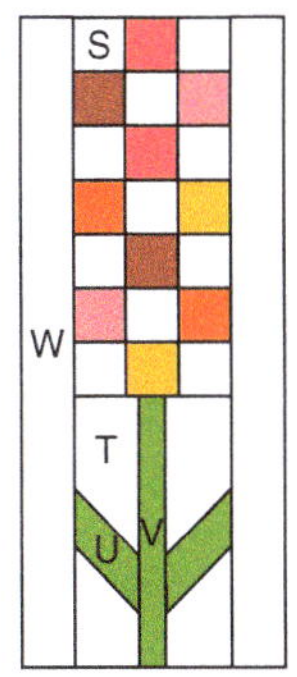

Flower
5" x 12" Finished Block
Make 16

MATERIALS

- ⅜ yard total assorted green prints*
- ⅞ yard floral print*
- 2½ yards cream print*
- 2 yards total assorted prints*
- 2 yards total assorted low-volume prints*
- ¾ yard binding fabric*
- 4⅓ yards backing fabric*
- 76" x 76" batting*
- Thread*
- Basic sewing tools and supplies

**Scrap fabrics from various collections by Moda Fabrics; Tuscany Silk batting from Hobbs Bonded Fibers; 50 wt. thread from Aurifil used to make sample. EQ8 was used to design this quilt.*

PROJECT NOTES

Read all instructions before beginning this project.

Sort assorted scraps into 12 different colors; label prints in each pile as Print 1 (house) and Print 2 (snail).

Stitch right sides together using a ¼" seam allowance unless otherwise specified.

Arrows indicate directions to press seams.

Materials and cutting lists assume 40" of usable fabric width for yardage.

WOF – width of fabric

HST – half-square triangle ⧅

QST – quarter-square triangle ⊠

Inspiration

"House blocks are one of my absolutely favorite blocks to make. I was inspired by watching snails moving their houses with them wherever they go for this humorous twist on normal house blocks." —Wendy Sheppard

CUTTING

FROM ASSORTED GREEN PRINTS CUT:

- 32 (1¾" x 2¾") U rectangles
- 16 (1" x 5½") V rectangles

FROM FLORAL PRINT CUT:

- 7 (3½" x WOF) strips, sew short ends to short ends, then subcut into:
  2 (3½" x 68½") Z strips and 2 (3½" x 63½") Y strips

FROM CREAM PRINT CUT:

- 11 (3½" x WOF) strips, sew short ends to short ends, then subcut into:
  2 (3½" x 63½") Y strips and 5 (3½" x 56½") X strips
- 32 (1¾" x 3½") T rectangles
- 32 (1¾" x 2¾") U rectangles
- 176 (1½") S squares
- 32 (1½" x 12½") W rectangles

FROM ASSORTED PRINT 1 PILES CUT:

- 12 sets of 1 (3½" x 6½") B, 2 (1½" x 3½") D, 2 (1½" x 6½") C, 1 (1½" x 4½") J, 1 (1½" x 2½") G and 1 (1½" x 2") H rectangles

FROM ASSORTED PRINT 2 PILES CUT:

- 12 sets of 1 (2½" x 12½") R rectangle, 1 (2") L and 3 (1½") O squares, and 1 (3½" x 5½") Q and 2 (1" x 3") N rectangles

FROM REMAINING ASSORTED PRINTS CUT:

- 160 (1½") S squares

FROM ASSORTED LOW-VOLUME PRINTS CUT:

- 12 sets of 1 (3" x 3½") P rectangle, 1 (2½" x 10½") M rectangle, 1 (2½" x 3½") E rectangle, 3 (2½") A squares, 1 (2" x 3½") I rectangle, 3 (2" x 2½") F rectangles, 1 (1½" x 10½") K rectangle, 1 (1½" x 6½") C rectangle, 1 (1½" x 2") H rectangle and 2 (1" x 3") N rectangles

FROM BINDING FABRIC CUT:

- 8 (2½" x WOF) binding strips

COMPLETING THE BLOCKS

Note: *For each Snail block, work with one Print 1 set, one Print 2 set and one low-volume set.*

1. Referring to Sew & Flip Corners on page 13, add one low-volume A square to the upper left corner of one B rectangle and then sew one C rectangle to the top to make one A-B-C unit (Figure 1). Make 12.

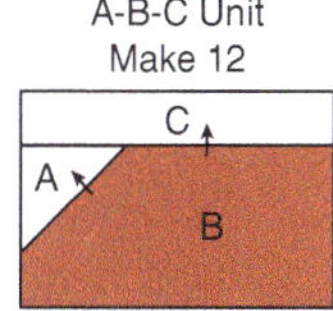

Figure 1

2. Sew together one each D and E rectangle, and draw a diagonal line on the wrong side as shown (Figure 2). Make 12.

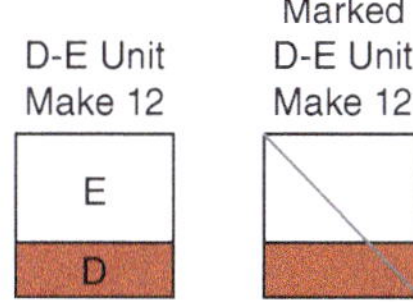

Figure 2

3. Using the sew-and-flip method, add the marked D-E unit to the A-B-C unit to make a roof unit (Figure 3). Make 12.

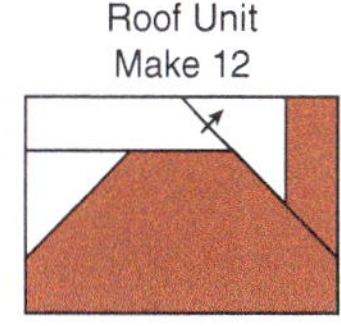

Figure 3

4. Sew F rectangles lengthwise to opposite sides of one G rectangle to make an F-G unit (Figure 4). Make 12.

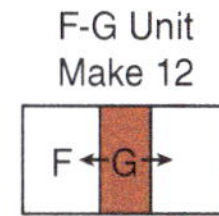

Figure 4

5. Sew one F rectangle to one H rectangle, and then sew to the left side of one D rectangle (Figure 5). Sew one I rectangle to the right side to make one D-F-H-I unit. Make 12.

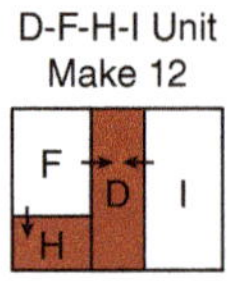

D-F-H-I Unit
Make 12

F D I H

Figure 5

6. Sew one F-G unit to the top and one F-G-H-I unit to the bottom of one J rectangle to make a house base unit (Figure 6). Make 12.

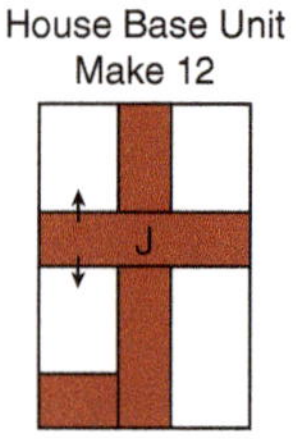

House Base Unit
Make 12

J

Figure 6

7. Sew C rectangles to opposite sides of one house base unit and then sew one roof unit to the top to make a house unit (Figure 7). Make 12.

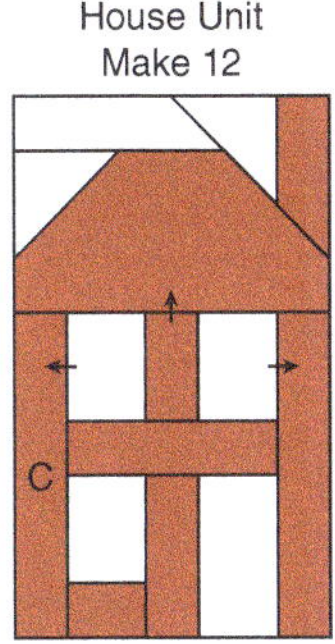

Figure 7

8. Sew one K rectangle to the left side and one M rectangle to the right side of the house unit. Using the sew-and-flip method, add an L square to the bottom corner of the M rectangle to make one House K-M unit (Figure 8). Make 12.

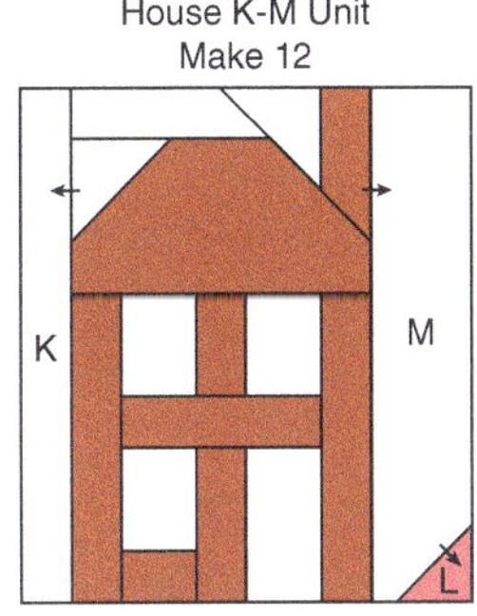

Figure 8

9. Sew together one each print and low-volume N rectangle and then use the sew-and-flip method to add an O square. Make a second unit in reverse. Sew together one H rectangle and one O square, and then sew N-O units to opposite sides to make one snail head unit (Figure 9). Make 12.

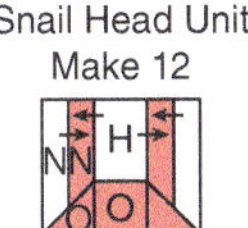

Figure 9

11. Sew one P rectangle to the top and one Q rectangle to the bottom of one snail head unit. Sew to the right side of the house K-M unit to make one snail top unit (Figure 10). Make 12.

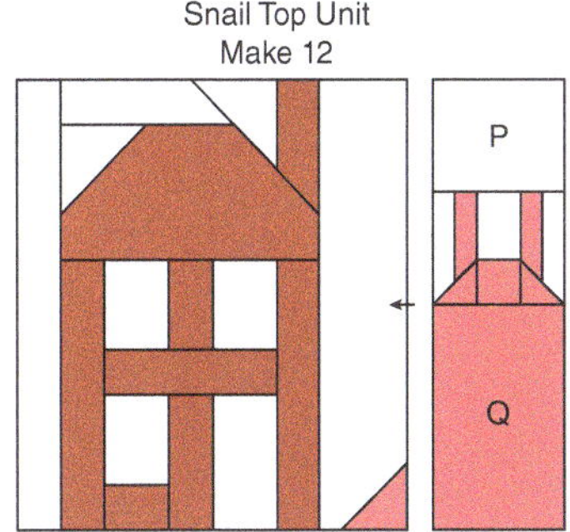

Figure 10

12. Using the sew-and-flip method, add A squares to the bottom corners of one R rectangle, and then sew to the snail top unit to make a Snail block (Figure 11). Make 12.

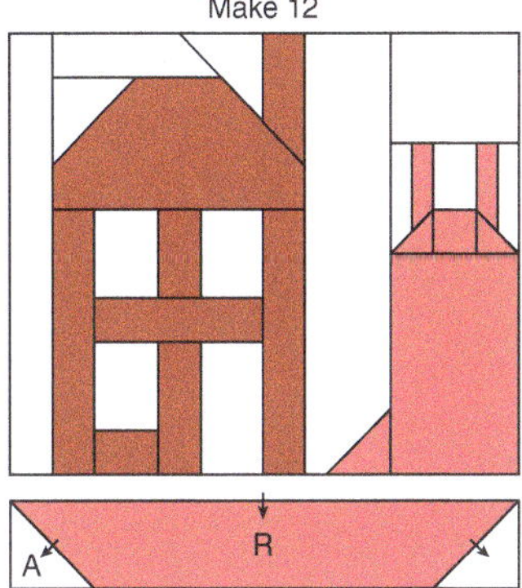

Figure 11

13. Lay out 11 cream S squares and 10 assorted print S squares into seven rows of three (Figure 12). Sew into rows and join the rows to make a 21-patch unit. Make 16.

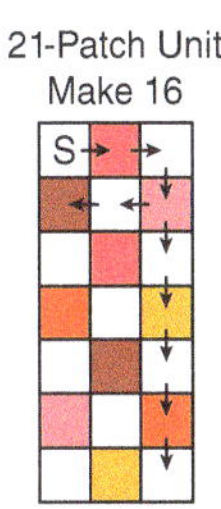

Figure 12

14. Using the sew-and-flip method, add one each low-volume T and U rectangle to one green U rectangle to make a T-U unit (Figure 13a). Make 16. In the same way, make 16 reverse T-U units (Figure 13b).

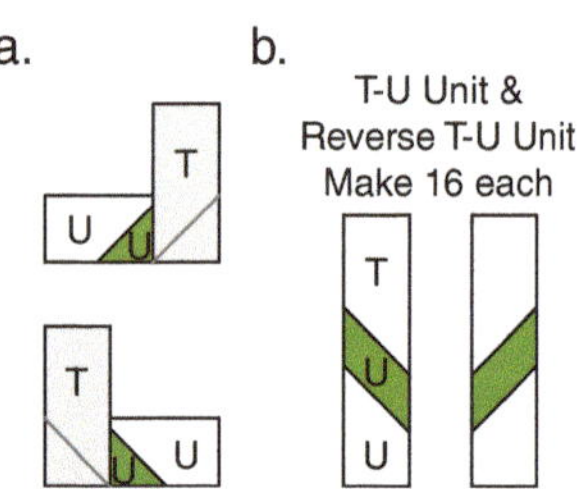

Figure 13

15. Sew one each T-U and reverse T-U units to opposite sides of one V rectangle to make a stem unit (Figure 14). Make 16.

Figure 14

16. Sew one 21-patch unit to the top of one stem unit and then sew W rectangles to both sides to make a Flower block (Figure 15). Make 16.

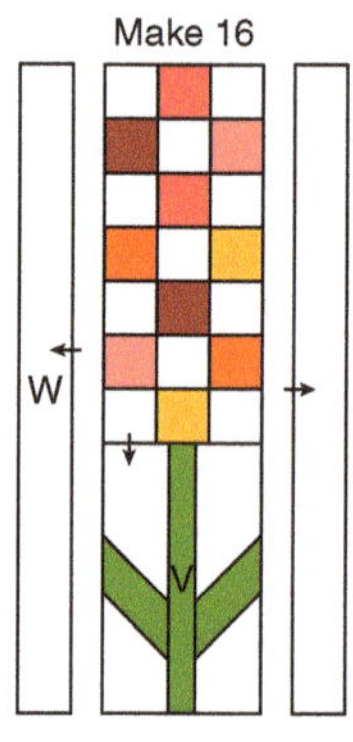

Figure 15

COMPLETING THE QUILT

1. Lay out four Flower blocks alternating with three Snail blocks and sew into a block row. Make four block rows.

2. Sew the four block rows together alternating with the five X strips. Sew cream Y strips to opposite sides.

3. Sew Y floral strips to opposite long sides of the quilt center and Z strips to the top and bottom to complete the quilt top.

4. Layer, baste, quilt as desired and bind referring to Quilting Basics. The photographed quilt was quilted with an overall loop design. ●

Who's Snailing Around Town?
Assembly Diagram 68" x 69"

WHOSE CACTI BLOOM?

Quilted by Darlene Szabo of Sew Graceful Quilting

This quilt is perfect for making a large visual impact by using up small pieces that you don't have the heart to toss.

SKILL LEVEL

Beginner

FINISHED SIZES

Quilt Size: 59" x 70"
Block Size: 10" x 10"
Number of Blocks: 30

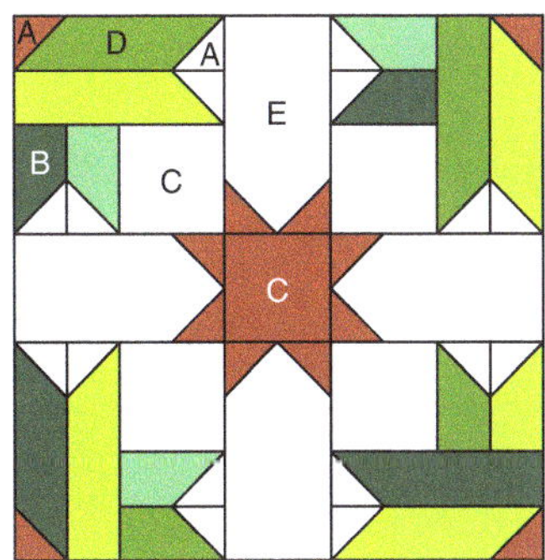

Cactus
10" x 10" Finished Block
Make 30

MATERIALS

- 1¼ yards total assorted red prints*
- 2¼ yards total assorted green prints*
- 3¾ yards total assorted low-volume prints*
- ⅝ yard binding fabric*
- 3⅜ yards backing fabric*
- 67" x 78" batting*
- Thread*
- Basic sewing tools and supplies

**Scrap fabrics from various collections by Moda Fabrics; Tuscany Silk batting from Hobbs Bonded Fibers; 50 wt. thread from used to make sample. EQ8 was used to design this quilt.*

PROJECT NOTES

Read all instructions before beginning this project.

Stitch right sides together using a ¼" seam allowance unless otherwise specified.

Arrows indicate directions to press seams.

Materials and cutting lists assume 40" of usable fabric width for yardage.

WOF – width of fabric
HST – half-square triangle ⧅
QST – quarter-square triangle ⊠

Inspiration

"I have designed many quilts with reds and greens, and I thought to myself, what is one more?" —Wendy Sheppard

CUTTING

FROM ASSORTED RED PRINTS CUT:

- 30 sets of 1 (2½") C square and 12 (1½") A squares
- 20 (1½") A squares

FROM ASSORTED GREEN PRINTS CUT:

- 240 (1½" x 4½") D rectangles
- 240 (1½" x 2½") B rectangles

FROM LOW-VOLUME PRINTS CUT:

- 7 (3" x WOF) strips, sew short ends to short ends, then subcut into:
  2 (3" x 65½") G strips and 2 (3" x 59½") H strips
- 120 (2½" x 4½") E rectangles
- 120 (2½") C squares
- 49 (1½" x 10½") F rectangles
- 480 (1½") A squares

FROM BINDING FABRIC CUT:

- 7 (2½" x WOF) binding strips

COMPLETING THE BLOCKS

Note: *Work with one red C and A square set per block.*

1. Referring to Sew & Flip Corners on page 13, add one low-volume A square to one B rectangle to make an A-B unit (Figure 1). Make 120 A-B units and 120 A-B reversed units. In the same way, make 120 each A-D units and A-D reversed units.

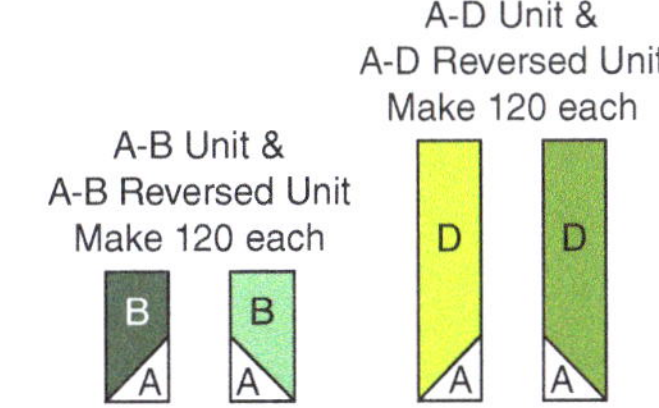

Figure 1

2. Sew together one each A-B unit and A-B reversed unit to make an A-B pair unit (Figure 2). Make 120.

Figure 2

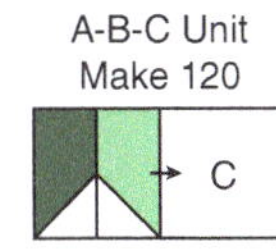

Figure 3

3. Sew one low-volume C square to the right side of one A-B pair unit to make an A-B-C unit (Figure 3). Make 120.

4. Sew together one each A-D unit and A-D reversed unit, and then use the sew-and-flip method to add one red A square to the upper left corner to make an A-D-A unit (Figure 4). Make 120.

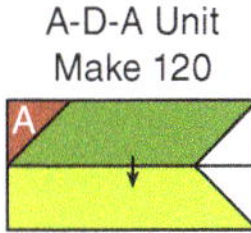

Figure 4

5. Sew one A-D-A unit to the top of one A-B-C unit to make a block corner unit (Figure 5). Make 120.

Figure 5

6. Using the sew-and-flip method, add two red A squares to the bottom corners of one low-volume E rectangle to make an A-E unit (Figure 6). Make 120.

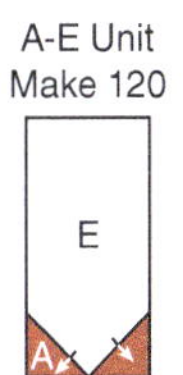

Figure 6

7. Lay out four block corner units, four A-E units and one red C square into three rows of three (Figure 7). Sew into rows and join the rows to make a Cactus block. Make 30.

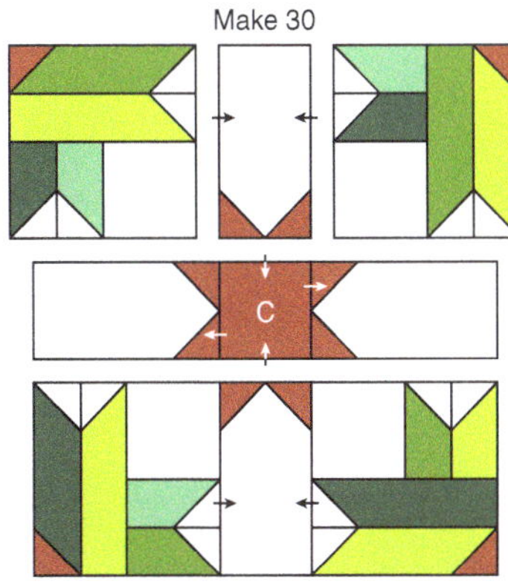

Figure 7

COMPLETING THE QUILT

1. Lay out five blocks alternating with four F rectangles and sew together to make a block row. Make six.

2. Lay out five F rectangles alternating with four red A squares and sew into a sashing row. Make five.

3. Sew block rows together alternating with sashing rows to complete the quilt center.

4. Sew G strips to opposite sides of the quilt center. Sew H strips to the top and bottom to complete the quilt top.

5. Layer, baste, quilt as desired and bind referring to Quilting Basics. The photographed quilt was quilted with an overall loop and swirl design. ●

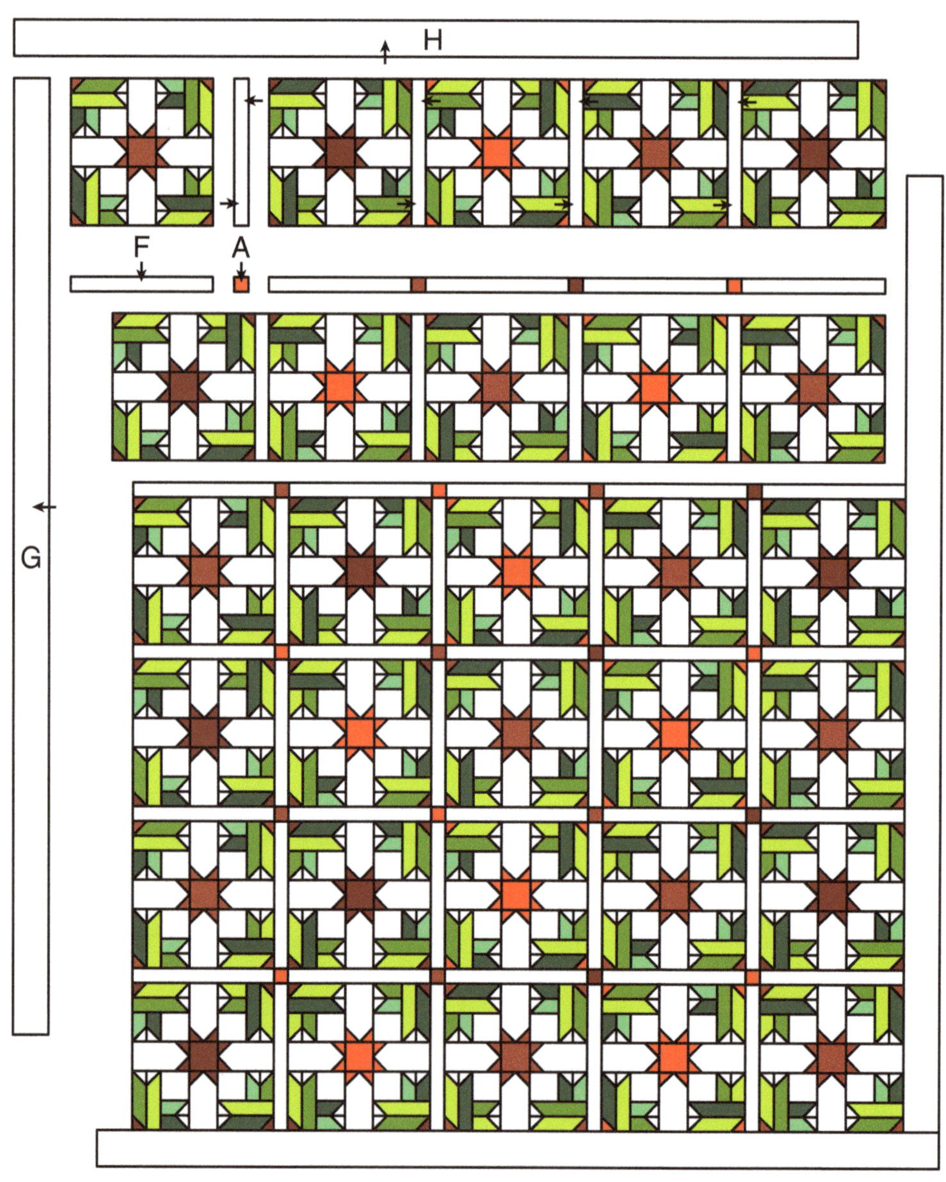

Whose Cacti Bloom?
Assembly Diagram 59" x 70"

WHO DREAMS IN COLOR?

Quilted by Darlene Szabo of Sew Graceful Quilting

Use up every fabric scrap in the bin to make this quilt, perfect for playing I spy with your little ones. Quilters will spy the gigantic Log Cabin block when the piecing is complete!

SKILL LEVEL

Confident Beginner

FINISHED SIZES

Quilt Size: 82" x 82"

Block Size: 4" x 4"

Number of Blocks: 319

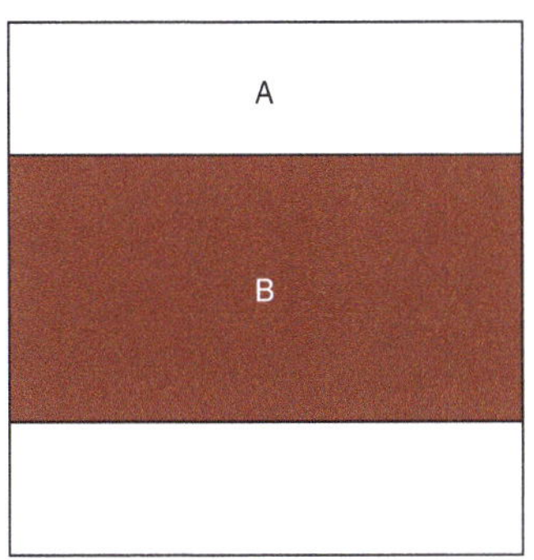

Rail Fence
4" x 4" Finished Block
Make 319

MATERIALS

- 3¾ yards low-volume prints*
- ½ yard red prints*
- ½ yard pink prints*
- ½ yard peach prints*
- ⅓ yard orange prints*
- ⅓ yard yellow prints*
- ⅓ yard medium green prints*
- ¼ yard dark green prints*
- 1 yard aqua prints*
- ¼ yard medium blue prints*
- ¼ yard dark blue prints*
- ¼ yard purple prints*
- ¼ yard brown prints*
- ¼ yard tan prints*
- ⅛ yard medium gray prints*
- ⅛ yard dark gray prints*
- ⅛ yard black prints*
- 1⅝ yards white-on-white print*
- 8 yards backing*
- 90" x 90" batting*
- Thread*
- Basic sewing tools and supplies

**Scrap fabrics from various collections by Moda Fabrics; Tuscany Silk batting from Hobbs Bonded Fibers; 50 wt. thread from Aurifil used to make sample. EQ8 was used to design this quilt.*

PROJECT NOTES

Read all instructions before beginning this project.

Stitch right sides together using a ¼" seam allowance unless otherwise specified.

Materials and cutting lists assume 40" of usable fabric width for yardage.

Arrows indicate directions to press seams.

WOF – width of fabric
HST – half-square triangle ⧄
QST – quarter-square triangle ⊠

Here's a Tip

If you prefer to bind your quilt with a single fabric instead of assorted aqua prints, you will need ¾ yard to cut nine (2½" x WOF) binding strips.

Inspiration

"I wanted to give the traditional Log Cabin block a fun twist by making one gigantic block from lots of little ones." —Wendy Sheppard

CUTTING

FROM LOW-VOLUME PRINTS CUT:

- 638 (1½" x 4½") A rectangles

FROM RED PRINTS CUT:

- 37 (2½" x 4½") B rectangles

FROM PINK PRINTS CUT:

- 35 (2½" x 4½") B rectangles

FROM PEACH PRINTS CUT:

- 33 (2½" x 4½") B rectangles

FROM ORANGE PRINTS CUT:

- 31 (2½" x 4½") B rectangles

FROM YELLOW PRINTS CUT:

- 29 (2½" x 4½") B rectangles

FROM MEDIUM GREEN PRINTS CUT:

- 25 (2½" x 4½") B rectangles

FROM DARK GREEN PRINTS CUT:

- 23 (2½" x 4½") B rectangles

FROM AQUA PRINTS CUT:

- 20 (2½" x 20") binding strips
- 21 (2½" x 4½") B rectangles

FROM MEDIUM BLUE PRINTS CUT:

- 19 (2½" x 4½") B rectangles

FROM DARK BLUE PRINTS CUT:

- 17 (2½" x 4½") B rectangles

FROM PURPLE PRINTS CUT:

- 13 (2½" x 4½") B rectangles

FROM BROWN PRINTS CUT:

- 11 (2½" x 4½") B rectangles

FROM TAN PRINTS CUT:

- 9 (2½" x 4½") B rectangles

FROM MEDIUM GRAY PRINTS CUT:

- 7 (2½" x 4½") B rectangles

FROM DARK GRAY PRINTS CUT:

- 5 (2½" x 4½") B rectangles

FROM BLACK PRINTS CUT:

- 4 (2½" x 4½") B rectangles

FROM WHITE-ON-WHITE PRINT CUT:

- 3 (4½" x WOF) strips, stitch short ends to short ends, then subcut into:
  1 (4½" x 52½") E strip and 1 (4½" x 56½") F strip
- 1 (4½" x 32½") D strip
- 1 (4½" x 28½") C strip
- 8 (3½" x WOF) strips, stitch short ends to short ends, then subcut into:
  2 (3½" x 76½") G and 2 (3½" x 82½") H border strips

Here's a Tip

When selecting low-volume prints for a block group (for example the 37 red blocks), look for those with small figures in similar or coordinating colors to the featured center prints of the blocks for extra color cohesion in the quilt.

COMPLETING THE BLOCKS

1. Sew A rectangles to the long sides of a red B rectangle to complete a red Rail Fence block measuring 4½" square from raw edge to raw edge (Figure 1). Make 37 total red blocks.

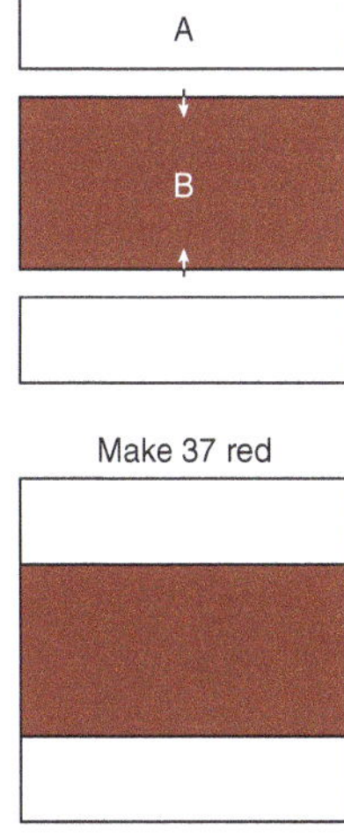

Figure 1

2. In the same way, use A and B rectangles to make 35 pink, 33 peach, 31 orange, 29 yellow, 25 medium green, 23 dark green, 21 aqua, 19 medium blue, 17 dark blue, 13 purple, 11 brown, 9 tan, 7 medium gray, 5 dark gray and 4 black blocks (Figure 2).

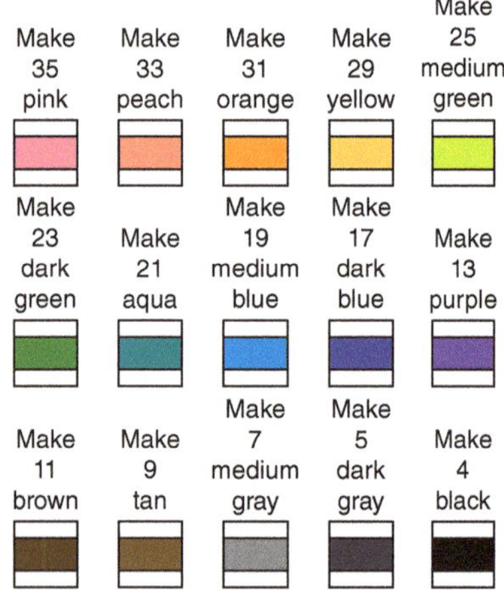

Figure 2

COMPLETING THE QUILT

1. Watch block orientation carefully throughout quilt assembly. Referring to the bottom right corner of the Assembly Diagram, sew two rows of two black blocks each. Join the rows to make a four-block square.

2. Join two dark gray blocks and then sew to the left side of the square. Join three dark gray blocks and then sew to the top to make a nine-block square.

3. Sew and add a strip of three medium gray blocks to the left side. Add a strip of four medium gray blocks to the top to make a 16-block square.

4. In the same way, add tan, brown and purple blocks to the square.

5. Sew the C strip to the left side. Sew the D strip to the top.

6. Add a strip of eight dark blue blocks to the left side. Add a strip of nine dark blue blocks to the top.

7. In the same way, add medium blue, aqua, dark green and medium green blocks to the square.

8. Sew the E strip to the left side. Sew the F strip to the top.

9. Add a strip of 14 yellow blocks to the left side. Add a strip of 15 yellow blocks to the top.

10. In the same way, add orange, peach, pink and red blocks to the square to complete the quilt center. Press.

11. Sew the G and H border strips to the quilt top in alphabetical order.

12. Layer, baste, quilt as desired and bind referring to Quilting Basics. The photographed quilt was quilted with an edge-to-edge ribbon design. ●

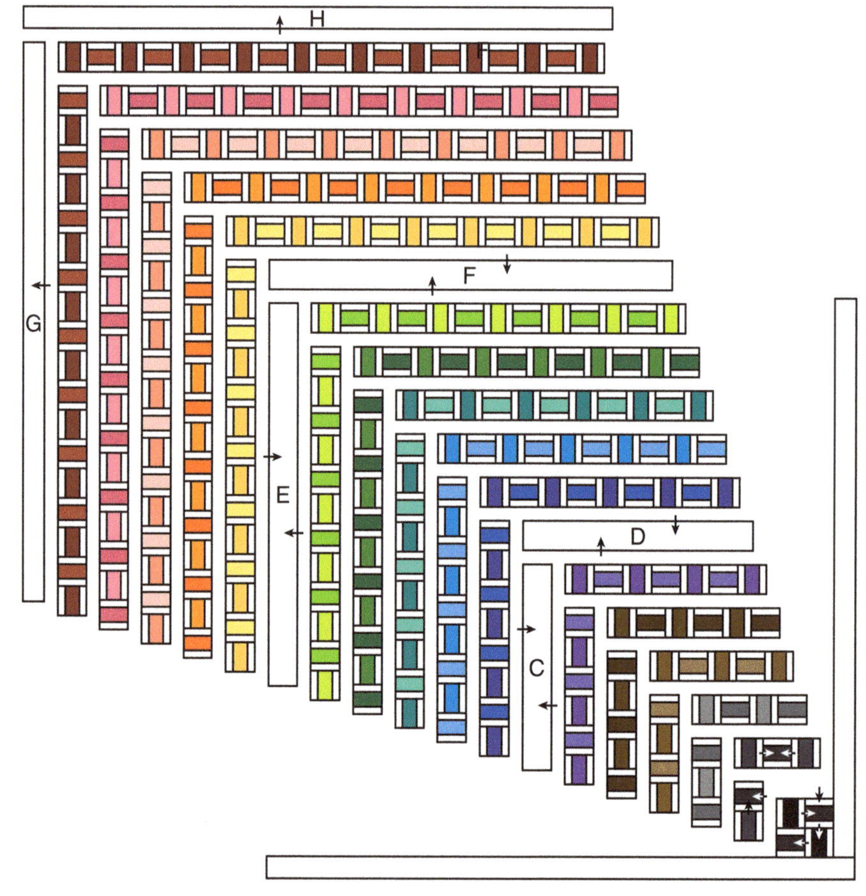

Who Dreams in Color?
Assembly Diagram 82" x 82"

WHO SPILLED THE ORANGE JUICE?

Quilted by Darlene Szabo of Sew Graceful Quilting

Using as many low volumes as possible makes the background sparkle in a quilt.

SKILL LEVEL

Beginner

FINISHED SIZES

Quilt Size: 80" x 80"

Block Size: 10" x 10"

Number of Blocks: 64

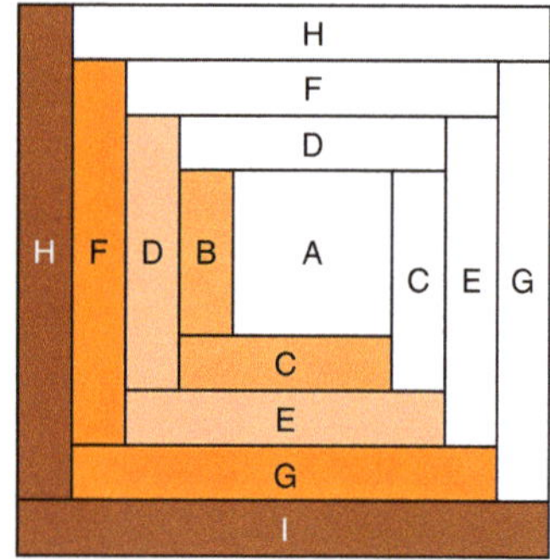

Log Cabin
10" x 10" Finished Block
Make 64

MATERIALS

- 4½ yards total low-volume scraps*
- 4¾ yards total orange scraps*
- 1 yard binding fabric*
- 8 yards backing fabric*
- 88" x 88" batting*
- Thread*
- Basic sewing tools and supplies

**Scrap fabrics from various collections by Moda Fabrics; Tuscany Silk batting from Hobbs Bonded Fibers; 50 wt. thread from Aurifil used to make sample. EQ8 was used to design this quilt.*

PROJECT NOTES

Read all instructions before beginning this project.

Stitch right sides together using a ¼" seam allowance unless otherwise specified.

Arrows indicate directions to press seams.

Materials and cutting lists assume 40" of usable fabric width for yardage.

WOF – width of fabric
HST – half-square triangle
QST – quarter-square triangle

CUTTING

FROM LOW-VOLUME FABRIC SCRAPS CUT:

- 80 (1½" x 9½") H rectangles
- 80 (1½" x 8½") G rectangles
- 80 (1½" x 7½") F rectangles
- 80 (1½" x 6½") E rectangles
- 80 (1½" x 5½") D rectangles
- 80 (1½" x 4½") C rectangles
- 80 (3½") A squares

FROM ORANGE FABRIC SCRAPS CUT:

- 80 (1½" x 10½") I rectangles
- 80 (1½" x 9½") H rectangles
- 80 (1½" x 8½") G rectangles
- 80 (1½" x 7½") F rectangles
- 80 (1½" x 6½") E rectangles
- 80 (1½" x 5½") D rectangles
- 80 (1½" x 4½") C rectangles
- 80 (1½" x 3½") B rectangles

FROM BINDING FABRIC CUT:

- 10 (2½" x WOF) binding strips

Inspiration

"Orange is not my normal color, but my orange stash had built up from the different autumn quilts I have made. So, I decided to mix up all the oranges with the low volumes for a sunshiny, bright and cheerful quilt to hang in my house during the fall season." —Wendy Sheppard

COMPLETING THE BLOCKS

1. Sew one orange B rectangle to the left side of one A square. Sew one orange C rectangle to the bottom, one low-volume C rectangle to the right side and one low-volume D rectangle to the top (Figure 1).

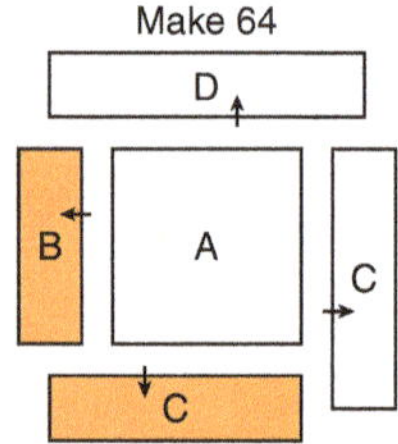

Figure 1

2. Continue adding the following pieces in the counterclockwise direction to complete one pieced block (Figure 2). Make a total of 80 blocks.

- orange D rectangle
- orange E rectangle
- low-volume E rectangle
- low-volume F rectangle
- orange F rectangle
- orange G rectangle
- low-volume G rectangle
- low-volume H rectangle
- orange H rectangle
- orange I rectangle

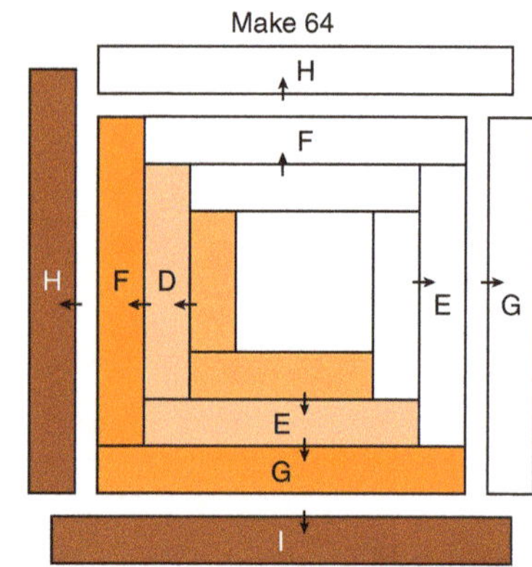

Figure 2

COMPLETING THE QUILT

1. Noting block orientations, lay out the blocks into eight rows of eight blocks. Sew blocks into rows and join the rows to complete the quilt top.

2. Layer, baste, quilt as desired and bind referring to Quilting Basics. The photographed quilt was quilted with an overall loop design. ●

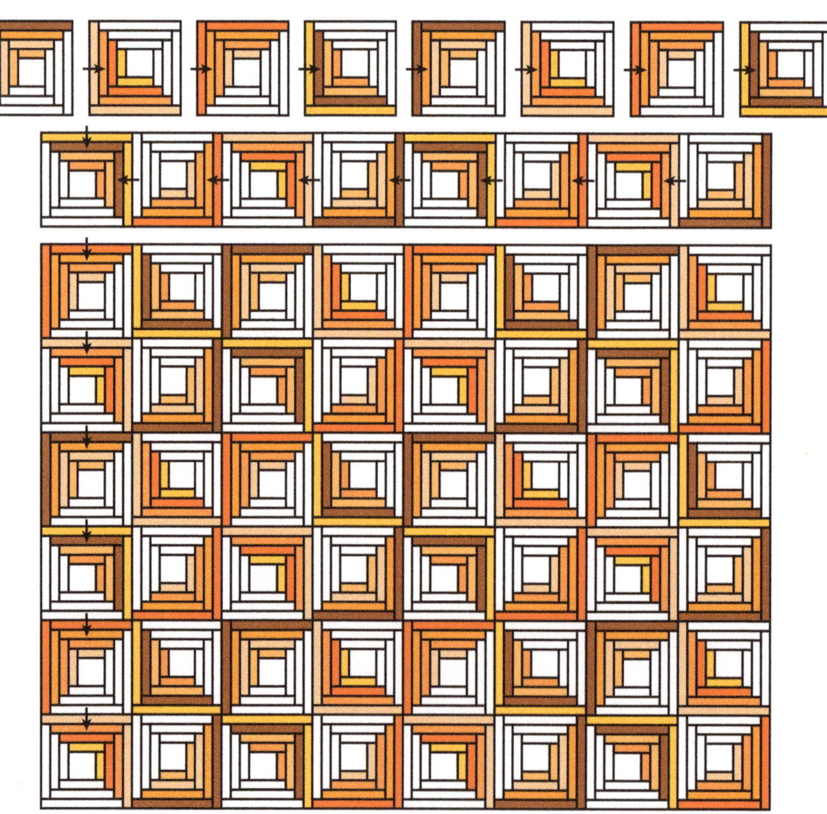

Who Spilled the Orange Juice?
Assembly Diagram 80" x 80"

Quilting Basics

The following is a reference guide. For more information, consult a comprehensive quilting book.

Quilt Backing & Batting

Cut your backing and batting 8" larger than the finished quilt-top size and 4" larger for quilts smaller than 50" square. ***Note:*** *Check with longarm quilter about their requirements, if applicable. For baby quilts not going to a longarm quilter 4"–6" overall may be sufficient.* If preparing the backing from standard-width fabrics, remove the selvages and sew two or three lengths together; press seams open. If using 108"-wide fabric, trim to size on the straight grain of the fabric. Prepare batting the same size as your backing.

Quilting

1. Press quilt top on both sides and trim all loose threads. ***Note:*** *If you are sending your quilt to a longarm quilter, contact them for specifics about preparing your quilt for quilting.*

2. Mark quilting design on quilt top. Make a quilt sandwich by layering the backing right side down, batting and quilt top centered right side up on flat surface and smooth out. Baste layers together using pins, thread basting or spray basting to hold. ***Note:*** *Tape or pin backing to surface to hold taut while layering and avoid puckers.*

3. Quilt as desired by hand or machine. Remove pins or basting as you quilt.

4. Trim batting and backing edges even with raw edges of quilt top.

Binding the Quilt

1. Join binding strips on short ends with diagonal seams to make one long strip; trim seams to ¼" and press seams open (Figure 1).

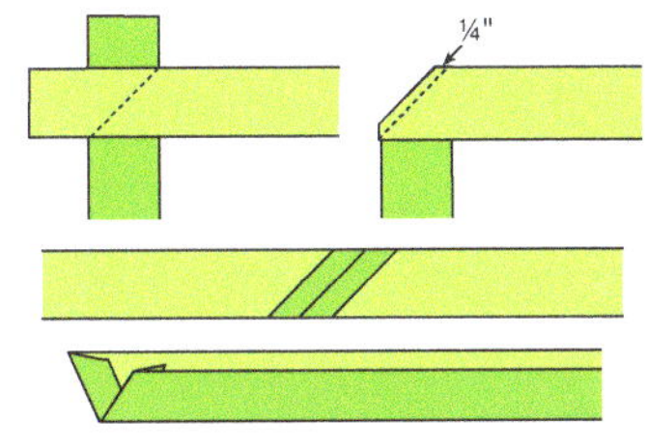

Figure 1

2. Fold ½" of one short end to wrong side and press. Fold the binding strip in half with wrong sides together along length, again referring to Figure 1; press.

3. Starting about 3" from the folded short end, sew binding to quilt top edges, matching raw edges and using a ¼" seam. Stop stitching ¼" from corner and backstitch (Figure 2).

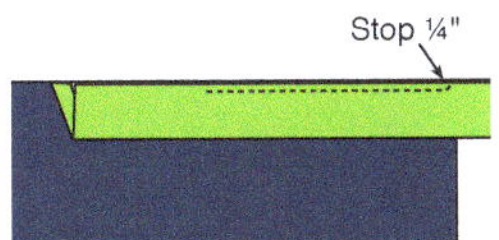

Figure 2

4. Fold binding up at a 45-degree angle to seam and then down even with quilt edges, forming a pleat at corner (Figure 3).

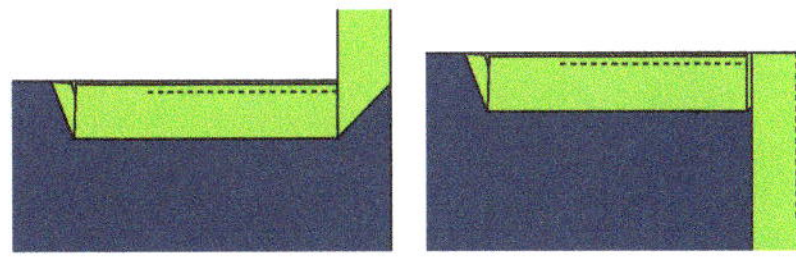

Figure 3

5. Resume stitching from corner edge as shown in Figure 3, down quilt side, backstitching ¼" from next corner. Repeat, mitering all corners, stitching to within 3" of starting point.

6. Trim binding, leaving enough length to tuck inside starting end and complete stitching (Figure 4).

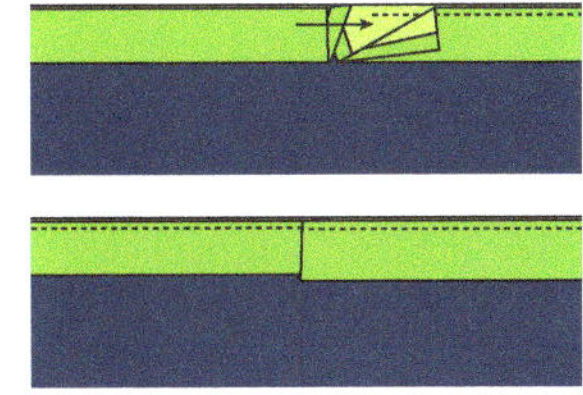

Figure 4

7. If stitching binding by hand, machine-sew binding to the front of the quilt and fold to the back before stitching. If stitching by machine, machine-sew binding to back of the quilt and fold to the front before stitching.

SPECIAL THANKS

Please join us in thanking the talented quilter whose work is featured in this collection.

Quilted by Darlene Szabo of Sew Graceful Quilting

SUPPLIES

We would like to thank the following manufacturers who provided materials to our designer to make sample projects for this book.

All projects: Scrap fabrics from various collections by Moda Fabrics; 50 wt. Aurifil thread; Tuscany Silk batting by Hobbs Bonded Fibers used to make sample.

Published by Annie's Attic, 306 East Parr Road, Berne, IN 46711. Printed in USA.

ISBN: 979-8-89253-397-3

3 4 5 6 7 8 9